ACTS: then and now

ACTS:

then and now

by Harvey H. Potthoff

JOINT COMMISSION ON EDUCATION AND CULTIVATION
BOARD OF MISSIONS OF THE METHODIST CHURCH
475 RIVERSIDE DRIVE
NEW YORK, N.Y. 10027

COVER: *The Church at Gelmeroda* by Lyonel Feininger. The Metropolitan Museum of Art,
New York City, George A. Hearn Fund,
1942

TITLE PAGE: *Whatever you do, do all for the glory of
God.* Wood Sculpture by Adlai S. Hardin,
The Interchurch Center, New York City

BOOK FORMAT: Mamie Harmon

APPROVED STUDY FOR WOMAN'S SOCIETIES OF
CHRISTIAN SERVICE AND WESLEYAN SERVICE GUILDS

To

the memory of my parents

The Reverend and Mrs. Henry A. Potthoff

RECOMMENDED MATERIALS

* ACTS: THEN AND NOW by Harvey H. Potthoff. $1.00
* GUIDE by Florence Hooper.   50 cents
* GOD'S WORK IN OUR TIME by Mrs. Coy P. Howe. Play. 14 characters.   30 cents; 4 for $1.00
* "THE GREATEST OF THESE . . ." by Mary Clark Tipps. Dramatic Worship Service. 3 characters.
     20 cents; 3 for 50 cents
* INTO ALL THE WORLD. The Book of Acts, illustrated. 8½ x 11 inches. RSV.[1]
* THE BEST GIFT. Illustrated booklet of the story of Pentecost (Acts 2:1-47).[1]
* PAUL, MAN OF PRAYER by Maud H. Lynch.   Free
* CHURCH IN THE WORLD by John Wesley. Prayer Card.
     25 for 50 cents

THE CHURCH AT GELMERODA [cover] color print, 23½ x 19⅛ inches. Order from Color Print Shop, Metropolitan Museum of Art, 5th Ave. at 82nd St., New York, N.Y.
   $1.00 plus 75 cents postage

* SERVICE CENTER, Board of Missions, The Methodist Church, 7820 Reading Road, Cincinnati, Ohio 45237

[1] Watch back cover of THE METHODIST WOMAN for release date and price.

BOOKS

See also "Books for Further Reading," pp. 113-119

* OUR MISSION TODAY, Tracey K. Jones, Jr. $1.00
THE BOOK OF ACTS IN HISTORY, Henry J. Cadbury. $3.50
EVANGELISM IN THE EARLY CHURCH, Stanley Brown. $2.00
A HISTORICAL INTRODUCTION TO THE NEW TESTAMENT, Robert M. Grant. $5.00
THE INTERPRETER'S BIBLE, Vol. 9, "The Acts of the Apostles."
   $8.75
THE MODERN READER'S GUIDE TO ACTS, Albert E. Barnett.
   50 cents

Order BOOKS from the Cokesbury Book Store serving your territory if not otherwise designated.

CONTENTS

INTRODUCTION,

THE PURPOSE OF THE STUDY

Why should anyone living in the space age of this technological twentieth century undertake the study of a book written approximately nineteen hundred years ago? Perhaps at the outset of our study it would be well to speak to that question.

There are three major reasons why a study of this justly famous work known as the Acts of the Apostles should be vital to us today. First, it relates an exciting story. One will look far and wide to find another work which equals the vivid account it gives of courageous persons engaged in vital living, expressing a deep commitment to a noble cause. The story is worth the reading for its own sake.

Christians, however, have a deeper reason for turning to the Book of Acts. Coming as it does out of the life of the early church, it throws much light on Christian beginnings and is thus an almost invaluable resource for the study of the apostolic age. Important insights into the life and problems confronting the early church help us grapple with our own sense of mission and community and with problems now confronting the church.

Although the primary purpose of the author may not have been that of recording history, the book nevertheless helps us to a deeper understanding of a crucial period in Christian history. He who would know the background out of which the modern church has come must have more than a superficial acquaintance with Acts.

The Scriptures we know as the Acts of the Apostles came out of the life of the early Christian church. Acts was written during the latter part of the first century. New Testament scholars generally agree that it originally comprised the second section of a two-volume work—the first part being what we know as the Gospel According to Luke. Thus, the whole work is frequently referred to as Luke-Acts. Luke, the first volume, deals with the life and ministry of Jesus; Acts, the second volume, relates the spread of the Christian movement in the years immediately following the life of Jesus.

Third, and perhaps most importantly, Acts speaks to our time. It has contemporary relevance for the church. It is a call to action under the living guidance of the Holy Spirit today. It is a call to discipleship and mission in the world today.

One of the most encouraging signs in Protestantism today is the new interest shown by lay men and women as well as theologians in the study of the nature and function of the church. In the midst of expanding church activities, more and more thoughtful people are asking the question, "Why?" What is the real purpose of the church? What makes the church different from other organizations? What is central and what is peripheral in its life? What are the community responsibilities of the church? How central should these be? What can we do to deepen the life of the church and make it more relevant to our time? It is indeed encouraging to note that more and more churchmen are asking questions such as these. If we sincerely seek answers to these questions, the church will be the stronger for it, and we shall be better churchmen, more faithful to the stewardship entrusted to us.

In seeking light on these matters we must look both to the past and the present. We must study the resources of church history, the great Christian literature including the devotional classics of the ages, the lives of Christian people, as well as contemporary knowledge, experience, anxieties, and needs. Biblical, theological, historical, sociological, psychological, and philosophical resources all have much to offer in a vital discussion of the church's function in today's world. Therefore, we turn to the Book of Acts as a major resource. Although the circumstances under which it was written were far different in many ways from those in which we do our living, we continue to find insight and inspiration in its pages, for it speaks to us as individuals and as institutions. It is this search for contemporary relevance in the Book of Acts which has determined the method used for our study.

THE METHOD OF STUDY

A great deal of research carried on by biblical scholars for many years has provided an ever-growing knowledge of the Book of Acts. The bibliography at the end of this volume lists some of the important writings which are available to the student who wishes to venture deeper into an understanding of the early Christian communities. In our first chapter we shall summarize some of the understandings we now have about the writing of Acts, its authorship, date, intended audience, and style.

Because we are seeking a deepened understanding of the *contemporary relevance* of Acts, we shall consider some of the great themes with which the book is concerned. We shall make a topical study. Each chapter has been divided into two main sections; the first section is historical and analytical, focused on the Book of Acts itself; the second section is concerned with the church of our time, and how the message of Acts speaks to the church of today, calling us to new depths of understanding and purpose.

Although each chapter is a unit by itself, it is necessary to study all the chapters, in order to see the book as a whole in proper perspective. The first chapter is entitled "An Over-All View of the Book of Acts." Successive chapters consider: "New Life in the Spirit," "The Church as Fellowship and Institution," "The Human Side of the Church," "The Church in Tension With the World," and "The Mission of the Church."

Since we must limit the topics to be dealt with, it is obvious that some matters of importance in the Acts of the Apostles will not be considered. It is hoped that this study will "whet the appetite" of the readers, leading them to go on to a further exploration of this remarkable New Testament book.

Acknowledgments. All quotations from the Bible are from the Revised Standard Version (copyrighted 1946, 1952, by the National Council of Churches of Christ in the United States of America).

The author is grateful to Dr. Martin Rist, Professor of New Testament and Christian History in the Iliff School of Theology, for reading the manuscript and making numerous suggestions, and to Mrs. Doyle Hauschulz for the typing of the manuscript.

Harvey H. Potthoff
Denver, Colorado

ONE:

an over-all view
of the Book of Acts

UPON UNDERTAKING A SERIOUS STUDY OF THE BOOK
of Acts we begin by asking: What is the book about?
What does the title mean? Is it a significant book in
the Christian heritage? Who was the author? When
and where was the book written? What was its
original purpose and to whom was it directed? Sec-
ondary questions may arise about style and organization of the contents.

After answering these questions, we shall be better
prepared to read the Book of Acts itself. And, having read Acts, we shall be in a position to ask: What
significance does this Scripture have for our own time?

ACTS IN PERSPECTIVE

New Testament scholars generally agree that what
we today know as the Gospel According to Luke and
the Acts of the Apostles were written by the same
author and were intended as two parts of a single

I

work. Luke narrates the events of the earthly career of Jesus, his death, resurrection, and departure; Acts picks up at this point with the words, "In the first book, O Theophilus, I have dealt with all that Jesus began to do and teach, until the day when he was taken up, after he had given commandment through the Holy Spirit to the apostle whom he had chosen."

Acts then deals with Jesus' farewell, his promise of the gift of the Holy Spirit, and his ascension. In vivid language and swiftly moving passages, the book reports early episodes in the Jerusalem church, the martyrdom of Stephen, the conversion of Saul, the work of Peter and the beginnings of Gentile conversions, the career of Paul, and the extension of the Christian mission. It ends with Paul in Rome.

The continuity of purpose and narrative, the reference to "the first book," the similarity in style and vocabulary of Luke and Acts,[1] all suggest that we are dealing with a two-volume work.

How Luke and Acts became separated is not known. However, we do know that early in the second century, Matthew, Mark, Luke, and John were published under the title "The Gospel." It may well be that the separation came about when Luke was given its place in the canonical Gospels leaving Acts as a separate work. Together Luke and Acts comprise more than one-fourth of the New Testament.

As Christians we begin to appreciate the importance of Acts when we realize that it is our major record of the apostolic age. Dealing as it does with

<hr>

[1] G. H. C. Macgregor, "Introduction," *The Interpreter's Bible*, Vol. 9 (Nashville: Abingdon Press, 1951), p. 7.

the generation immediately following Jesus' earthly ministry, it includes matters considered in no other existing writing. The letters of Paul are closely related to many of the concerns of Acts, but there is much in Acts pertaining to Paul's own career and to the rise and expansion of Christianity not covered by Paul's letters. For example, only in Acts do we find a detailed account of Paul's conversion (chapter 9); the mission of Paul and Barnabas to Cyprus (chapter 13); Paul's speech in the Areopagus (chapter 17); Paul's arrest (chapter 21); Paul's trip to Rome (chapters 27 and 28).

Yet, a perceptive reader is likely to be fascinated and bewildered by what Acts leaves out; so much is left to be inferred. There is only one brief reference to Christianity in Galilee (9:31). Apart from passages dealing with Peter, and to a lesser extent with John, James, and Judas, we are given no individual information on the Twelve.

Although Peter and Paul are the central figures in Acts, many questions which arouse curiosity about them are left unanswered. Peter disappears from the narrative without explanation. No reference is made to the last days of Paul, although he was almost certainly dead at the time of the writing of Acts.[1]

---

[1] "If he [author of Acts] was primarily an apologist for Christianity, and the origin and progress of the Gentile Mission his main theme, then the details of Paul's death were as irrelevant as the details of the great Apostle's birth and his life as a Jew. Moreover, after taking considerable pains to show that throughout Paul's career as a Christian he had been consistently vindicated by every properly constituted civil court before which he had been brought, to conclude with an account of his execution in Rome must have seemed to Luke a stultification of his purpose." H. F. D. Sparks, *Hastings' Dictionary of the Bible*. Rev. ed. by Frederick C. Grant and H. H. Rowley (New York: Chas. Scribner's Sons, 1963), p. 600b.

And if a major purpose of the author was to account historically for the rise and spread of the Christian movement, why has he nothing to say about the spread of the gospel to Egypt? Considerations such as these indicate that the author may have had other purposes in mind than the simple recording of historical events.

THE TITLE

When or by whom the title "The Acts of the Apostles" was first given to this writing is not known. In our own time the title is sometimes shortened to "Acts" or to the "Book of Acts." This abbreviation is found in one of the older Greek manuscripts. In one sense the Acts of the Apostles is not an appropriate title because the book has little or nothing to say about some of the apostles (The Twelve) but concentrates primarily on Peter and Paul.

The word "apostles" may possibly be in the plural in order to distinguish this writing from apocryphal (non-canonical) works dealing with individuals and bearing such titles as "The Acts of Paul" and "The Acts of Peter." [1]

One scholar has suggested that it might well have been called the Acts of Peter and Paul. Acts certainly reflects the attitude of the second-century church in

----

[1] "The sequel most obviously demanded by the Book of Acts is some account of what became of Paul." [It was written] "by a Christian elder in Asia ... who about A.D. 160-70 had come to feel that the Pastoral Letters exaggerated Paul's views on the place of women in the church and needed to be corrected." [It features aversion to marriage and indorsement of woman's place in teaching.] Edgar J. Goodspeed, *A History of Early Christian Literature* (Chicago: University of Chicago Press, 1942), p. 98.

giving Peter and Paul a unique status among the apostles. Following the account in the first chapter of the naming of Matthias to take the place of Judas, there is no further reference to Matthias, and only three of the disciples, Peter, James, and John, are mentioned again. If the original two-volume work which today is often referred to as Luke-Acts ever had a name, we do not know what it was.

It seems clear therefore that the real purpose of the work was not to give a comprehensive account of the activities of the Twelve. Professor James Moffatt, biblical scholar, once suggested that an appropriate title for the book might have been "How They Brought the Good News to Rome." While the author seems indeed much concerned with bringing Paul to Rome in his account, it should be remembered that Christianity had made its way to the imperial capital before Paul's arrival there (2:10; 28:15).

The word "acts" is surely appropriate, for this book is brimful of action and adventure. One cannot read it without being caught up in the current of vitality and movement it recreates. There was nothing lazy or halfhearted about its central characters!

PURPOSE AND INTENDED AUDIENCE

Whatever the primary purpose of the author, his heart was obviously in his writing. As one reads he becomes caught up in the author's excitement about the Christian movement, his commitment to its message, his hope for its future, and his admiration for its leaders. The words "joy" and "rejoice" appear frequently in Luke-Acts. It is evident that, even in times of trial, the life of the early church was a life of joy, faith, hope, and prayer (2:46; 5:41; 13:52; 15:3 and 31).

New Testament scholarship has developed a number of theories as to the *purpose* of Acts.[1] *One theory* is that the author was primarily interested in writing a book of history, tracing the spread of Christianity from Jerusalem to Rome. That the author deals with important historical materials is evident. However, there are reasons to doubt that the writing of history was the author's primary purpose. For example, he omits much relevant information about his central figures, Peter and Paul, and others of historical significance (see TEXT, pp. 4-5). Moreover, it is difficult to harmonize some of the material in Acts pertaining to Paul with Paul's own accounts in his letters. (Compare 9:20-29; 11:29-30; 15:1-29 with Gal. 1:15-2:14.) Thus, while it appears that the author was dealing with highly important matters relating to the history of the early church, his primary interest was not the writing of history, for history's sake. There appears to have been a deeper concern.

A *second theory* is that the book was written for a religious purpose—to witness to the work of the Holy Spirit in the early church. It is easy to understand how this theory could arise because from the first chapter on we find repeated references to the work of the *Holy Spirit,* to which we shall specifically turn our attention in the next chapter. Obviously the author *was*

[1] G. H. C. Macgregor, *The Interpreter's Bible,* Vol. 9, p. 15.

concerned with witnessing to the reality and power of the Holy Spirit. However, a careful reading of the Book of Acts suggests that he had more in mind, for he introduces material which would seem to indicate further interests. Important as the work of the Holy Spirit is in the book, it does not exhaust the meaning or purpose of Acts.

A *third theory* suggests that the author was concerned with presenting an apology for, or defense of, Christianity—directed to critics or potential converts. That the Christian movement is presented in a most favorable light, there can be no doubt. It is presented as being divinely inspired and led.

> "So in the present case I tell you, keep away from these men and let them alone; for if this plan or this undertaking is of men, it will fail; but if it is of God, you will not be able to overthrow them. You might even be found opposing God!"
>
> Acts 5:38-39

The amazing success of the mission, and Paul's work in particular, is emphasized (6:7; 9:31; 12:24; 16:5; 19:20; 28:30). The solidarity of the Christian community is stressed. These would suggest that the author had an apologetic interest in mind.

This suggestion is closely related to the *fourth theory* which has been developed—a theory which is widely held: that a purpose of the book—if not *the* major purpose—was political in nature, namely, the interpretation of the Christian movement in a favorable light to Roman authorities.

Several types of evidence have been brought forward in support of this political theory. The first has to do with the person Theophilus, to whom both the Gospel of Luke and the Book of Acts are addressed. We do not know who he was; the name itself (meaning "Beloved of God"), was a common one in the ancient world. However, it is significant that in the Gospel of Luke he should be addressed as "most excellent" Theophilus. He appears to have been a person of prestige. The words "most excellent" are used only three times in Acts—twice in addressing Felix and once in addressing Festus, both of whom were Roman governors (23:26 KJV; and 24:2 RSV; and 26:25 RSV).

If Theophilus were indeed a Roman provincial official, suspicious of Christianity, and if the writer's intended audience included Theophilus and other officials like him, we would have an explanation for much of the material found in Acts which is not satisfactorily accounted for in terms of the other theories. The emphasis on Paul's Roman citizenship (23:27), the frequent references to Roman officials, the exoneration of Pilate from responsibility for Jesus' death (3:13), Gallio's dismissal of charges against Paul (18:12-16), the failure of various procurators and proconsuls to convict Paul (24:22; 25:12), and the efforts to integrate Christianity into Roman life as in the synchronization of Christian events with the Roman chronology (Luke 2:1; 3:1), all take on added significance in the light of this theory of the purpose of Acts.

It is evident that several New Testament books were written against the background of trouble or potential trouble with civil authority: Hebrews, Luke-

Acts, Revelation, First Peter. In time the Christian assertion of supreme allegiance to Jesus Christ raised questions about the loyalty of Christians to the emperor. When the refusal of Christians to engage in emperor worship became a major issue cannot be stated with precision; it was probably some time after the writing of Acts. However, Christians were persecuted during the reign of Domitian in which period Acts was probably written. Thus, some governmental authorities were suspicious and hostile toward the new religious movement. It was essential that a favorable interpretation of Christianity be directed to responsible authorities. It may well be that Acts was written for this purpose.

It is significant that the book emphasizes that Christianity is not an alien movement, but indigenous to the empire; that Christianity is the "true Judaism" (2:46; 3:1; 5:30-31; 13:15; 15:15-17; 17:3; 18:19; 21:20, 26; 22:3) and thus is entitled to legal recognition and protection; that Christianity is indeed of God and has enjoyed the special blessing of God from its beginnings (1:9-11; 4:31; 5:19; 8:26; 10:3-19; 12:6-11). The working of miracles (2:43; 3:6; 4:10; 6:8; 8:6; 9:34), the unhappy ending of those who oppose Christianity (12:23), and the power of the gospel are all cited as evidence of divine sanction of the Christian movement.

Running throughout the book is the note of confidence in the divinely directed spread of the movement. Accounts of the enlarging outreach of Christianity are found in such passages as: 1:9 through 6:7 (Jerusalem); 6:8 through 9:31 (Palestine); 9:32

through 12:24 (Antioch); 12:25 through 16:5 (Asia Minor); 16:6 through 19:20 (southeastern Europe); 19:21 through 28:31 (Rome). Summary statements of Christianity's growth following the command to witness in Acts 1:8 are found in 6:7, 9:31, 12:24, 16:5, 19:20, and 28:31. If indeed a major purpose of the author was to present a favorable interpretation of Christianity to Roman officialdom, he performed this task with remarkable skill. To sum up, Acts displays a combination of historical, religious, apologetic, and political interests. No reader could lay aside this amazing book unimpressed.

THE AUTHOR, TIME AND PLACE OF WRITING

While we can infer much concerning the author of Acts, we do not know with certainty who he really was. Indeed much research has gone into this question and several theories have been advanced. (Every major book dealing with Luke-Acts discusses its authorship. Attention is called to the bibliography at the end of this volume which lists sources giving more extended treatments of the question.)

Many, if not most, New Testament scholars believe that one person was primarily responsible for the writing and (or) the compiling of Luke and Acts. The opening lines of Luke suggest that the author received some of his information from "those who from the beginning were eyewitnesses and ministers of the word" (Luke 1:2). This statement implies that he himself was not an eyewitness. Whether or not these opening words in Luke were intended as an introduction to the two-volume Luke-Acts cannot be definitely said.

Of particular interest are the so-called "we-passages" which involve Paul's journeys and sea voyages (16:10-18; 20:5-16; 21:1-18; 27:1 through 28:16). Since the first person plural is used in these passages, the natural conclusion is that the author himself was a companion of Paul. Yet one cannot be absolutely sure, for authors sometimes use the first person plural as a literary device to describe more vividly events in which they took no part.

If, however, we assume that the author of these passages was an actual companion of Paul, the question as to who he was still remains unanswered. The author most frequently suggested is Luke. In Paul's letters references are made to many companions, including Luke who is mentioned in Colossians 4:14 and Philemon 24. In Colossians Luke is referred to as "the beloved physician." That Luke may be considered as a possible author of the "we-passages" is obvious; that he actually was the author is certainly not definite. In II Timothy 4:11 we find the words "Luke alone is with me." If these were the actual words of Paul they would strengthen the case for the Lukan authorship of the "we-passages." However, many New Testament scholars are now convinced that Paul was not the author of I and II Timothy.

Moreover, several arguments have been voiced in opposition to the theory that Luke was the author of Acts. Apparently the author of Acts was not familiar with Paul's letters and presumably Luke would have known them. It is difficult to reconcile some accounts in Acts with what we find in Paul's letters.

On the other hand it may be argued that Paul's letters might not have been collected and available at the time of the writing of Acts. Edgar J. Goodspeed, in his book *The Meaning of Ephesians,* suggests that the publication of Acts, with its thrilling account of Paul's missionary journeys, actually inspired the collection and publication of the apostle's letters.[1] Variations in the reporting of various events may be due to differences in purpose of writing. It is conceivable that the introductory statement in Luke, chapter 1, was not intended to cover Acts—or that the author may simply have meant that "among" his sources were certain eyewitnesses.

Thus, we do not know with certainty who actually wrote the material with which we are dealing. It is also possible that more than one person was involved in the writing and compiling of Luke-Acts. Conceivably, the "we-passages" may have been incorporated into the writing of Acts by a second person. There may have been several steps in the writing and compiling of Luke-Acts: the writing of Luke; the writing of the "we-passages" (perhaps as a travel diary); the inclusion of these passages into a fuller narrative dealing with Paul; the addition of still further materials —including those dealing with Peter—to form the present Book of Acts; and finally the addition of Acts to Luke. We do not know.

Actually it is not important that we know with cer-

---

[1] See Francis W. Beare, "Ephesians, Introduction," *The Interpreter's Bible,* Vol. 10, p. 602.

tainty who the author was. We do know from his writing of his commitment to the Christian movement and through him we gain invaluable understanding of certain aspects of the church in the apostolic age. Because of his work we can obtain a deepened understanding not only of what the early church was but of what the modern church is called to be. In many ways, Acts speaks to our time.

Such evidence as we have indicates that Acts was written after A.D. 60, probably in the latter part of the first century. Various theories have been advanced as to the place of writing: Ephesus; Rome; Corinth or its environs; others.

STYLE AND ORGANIZATION

The Book of Acts is unique among the Christian writings of its time. Imitations of it followed its publication, but it marked a distinctive form of writing at the time of its appearance.

The author gives evidence of unusual literary artistry. His style is varied, influenced perhaps by the different sources he used, adapted and fitted skillfully to the particular situation he described. All in all, it is more "cultivated" than that found in most other Greek biblical writings.

The modern reader may be surprised to realize that the author of Acts does not follow a strictly chronological pattern in organizing his materials. He seems more interested in centering what he has to say around persons and geographical areas. [This is also done in Genesis and other books in the Old Testament.

See *Genesis: Beginnings of the Biblical Drama* by Charles F. Kraft, pp. 109-10.] The materials consist of reported events, summaries of various kinds, and numerous speeches. The speeches make up between one-fourth and one-third of Acts.

The speeches presented are attributed to Peter, James, Stephen, and Paul. It is, of course, most unlikely that the author had reliable reports of such speeches before him at the time of writing. We must, therefore, accord to the author himself considerable credit for both their form and content as they presently appear in the book. Moreover, the speeches significantly reveal some of the central ideas with which he is concerned.

In terms of broad outline we may divide the Book of Acts into three parts: chapters one through seven describe the development of the Christian movement in Jerusalem; chapters eight through twelve deal with the spread of the Christian movement to Samaria, Damascus, Joppa, Caesarea, and Antioch; chapters thirteen through twenty-eight record Paul's mission in Asia Minor and Greece, bringing him at last to Rome.

Another organization of the material which one will note in reading Acts is under the following topics: the church in Jerusalem (1:1 through 6:7); the expansion through Palestine (6:8 through 9:31); the expansion of the movement to Antioch (9:32 through 12:24); the expansion to Asia Minor and Galatia (12:25 through 16:5); the expansion to Europe (16:6 through 19:20); the further expansion of the church with Paul's final arrival in Rome (19:21 through 28:31).

SUGGESTIONS FOR READING

The ideal way to read the Acts of the Apostles is to read the entire book at one time. If that is not possible, it would be helpful to follow the divisions of the book as indicated above, reading it in three or six sections. In any event, there is no substitute for reading the book itself. It is now suggested that the reader do exactly that before proceeding further.

TWO:

new life in the spirit

ONE OF THE DISTINGUISHING FEATURES OF THE BOOK
of Acts is its emphasis upon the gift and work of the
Holy Spirit. Let us, then, consider the interpretation
and significance of the Holy Spirit in the early church,
then go on to consider the meaning of the new life in
the Spirit for our own lives and in our own time.

THE HOLY SPIRIT IN ACTS

A Story of Changed Lives. Acts is indeed a story of
lives empowered and made new. The same Peter
who in Luke 22:54-62 is portrayed as denying Jesus
emerges in Acts witnessing boldly to the lordship of
Jesus (2:14-40). Saul, the persecutor of Christians
(9:1-2), becomes Paul, the great Christian missionary
(9:20-22). Barnabas, the Seven, and others are empowered in remarkable ways to do what they could
never have done in their own strength. The disciples
who had known despair come to a new outlook and

17

hope. They now look to the future in expectancy and confidence. There is a profound, inner transformation. The disciples are changed people.

The Christian community is portrayed as one of triumphant spirit. The note of joy and gladness permeates the Book of Acts. Christians are seen facing danger and persecution in fortitude. They witness in boldness. Theirs is the power to endure in hope and to work in courage and gladness.

What is the explanation of this transformation? To find the answer as it is given in Acts we must turn to the theology of the book and more especially to its interpretation of the Holy Spirit. It is in the gift and activity of the Holy Spirit that we find the explanation of the changed lives.

The Theology of Acts. Acts is not, and was not intended to be, a work on systematic, or formal, theology. However, the book as a whole presupposes certain theological concepts and points of view. We need to comprehend the theological perspective of Acts if we are to understand much of what the author has to say throughout his book.

A number of the speeches—particularly those attributed to Peter and Paul—are especially important in setting forth the underlying theological ideas of Acts. Special reference might well be made to the following speeches by Peter in this connection: at Pentecost (2:14-40); in Solomon's Portico (3:12-26); before the Sanhedrin (4:8-12); at the house of Cornelius (10:34-43); to the Jewish Christians at Jerusalem (11:5-17); at a Jerusalem council (15:7-11).

The addresses of particular theological interest attributed to Paul are the following: to Jews at Antioch of Pisidia (13:16-41 and 46-47); to Gentiles at Athens (17:22-31).

God, according to the theology of Acts, is creator of the world and everything in it. He is the giver of life. God is in control of history, possessing both power and foreknowledge. God is both judge and provider.

Whereas God has declared himself in times past, he has more recently preached the good news of peace through Jesus Christ. God's climactic and decisive action has been in raising Jesus from the dead. The Resurrection vindicates Jesus' message of repentance and points toward his return as judge of the living and the dead. In anticipation of future judgment all men are called to repentance. God has made Jesus both Lord and Christ (Messiah). Men are now called to repent, not only for their misdeeds, but for their failure to acknowledge Jesus as Lord and Christ.

Thus, in Acts, the emphasis is not so much upon the Jesus of history as upon the Christ of faith (3:16 and 26; 20:21). Forgiveness of sins and freedom from all that the law cannot free one from are promised to those who repent and believe. Salvation is through Jesus Christ alone (4:12).

A number of passages in Acts refer to the preaching of the kingdom of God (1:3; 8:12; 14:22; 19:8; 28:23 and 30-31). Whether the author of Acts thought of the kingdom of God as did Jesus, or whether he thought of it more in apocalyptic terms, cannot be stated with certainty. However, references throughout Acts to the return of Christ in judgment indicate that the apocalyptic pattern was in the author's thinking.

In the first chapter of Acts we have the report of Jesus' ascension to heaven. Attendant upon the ascension two promises were given to the apostles: the first by Jesus himself that "you shall receive power when the Holy Spirit has come upon you" (1:8); and the second by two men in white robes that Jesus would return in the same manner as that by which he went into heaven (1:10-11). These promises bring us to the consideration of Acts' interpretation of the gift and activity of the Holy Spirit.

Biblical Backgrounds. In order to understand what is said in Acts concerning the Holy Spirit, it is well first to note some of the ways in which the work of spirit has been understood in earlier thought. In primitive religion we find the belief in a mysterious power which may enter a person and make him its instrument. Persons in a state of ecstasy or high enthusiasm were sometimes regarded as being possessed by a spirit.

There are numerous references in the Old Testament to the Spirit of God or the Holy Spirit. (Incidentally, the term "Holy Ghost" in the King James Version has precisely the same meaning as "Holy Spirit" in the Revised Standard Version.) Apparently the earliest Hebrew understanding of the Spirit of Yahweh was not far removed from primitive thought; it was believed to be a force that comes suddenly and without explanation upon individuals. The Hebrew word for spirit (*rûaḥ*) means "wind"—and in earliest times there was believed to be a wind-like force which would come upon persons, producing perceptible results, granting them unusual physical strength, wisdom, or foresight. In time this force, akin to breath or an emanating force, came to be associated with Yahweh. The Spirit was sometimes said to come upon a person, to rush upon him, or to clothe him. The stories of the judges, King Saul, Samson, and Bezalel all reflect early thinking about the effects of spirit.

At a somewhat later period the work of the Spirit was associated with prophetic frenzy. Elisha asked and received a double portion of Elijah's spirit. Prophets came to be understood as Spirit-possessed, and their prophecies as Spirit-inspired. Exalted physical and mental states were attributed to the working of the Spirit. In time divine impulse and knowledge came to be known as the result of the Spirit's presence. Sometimes Old Testament references to Spirit seem to imply a personal being and on other occasions the suggestion seems to be that of an impersonal inbreathing.

Numerous references to spirit are found in the Old Testament with variations of meaning. The Spirit of God is associated on occasion with creation, inspiration, holiness, fertility, varied blessings. Generally speaking Old Testament references to the Spirit of God refer to the divine presence and activity in the world.

In Joel we find the anticipation of a time when God would pour out his Spirit *on all flesh:*

> "And it shall come to pass afterward,
>   that I will pour out my spirit on all flesh;
> your sons and daughters shall prophesy,

> your old men shall dream dreams,
> and your young men shall see visions.
> Even upon the menservants and maidservants
> in those days, I will pour out my spirit."
>
> Joel 2:28-29

In the teachings of Jesus we find relatively little reference to the work of the Spirit, although there are Gospel references suggesting that Jesus' work is done in the power of the Spirit. Whereas the disciples believed Jesus to be inspired of the Spirit, they did not claim this for themselves during his ministry. In Mark 12:36 and Matthew 22:43 Jesus uses a Rabbinic expression relating the Spirit to the writing of the Scriptures. In Luke 4:18 the Gospel writer portrays Jesus quoting Isaiah 61:1 as referring to his own ministry: "The Spirit of the Lord is upon me. . . ."

Paul speaks frequently of the Spirit, the Spirit of Christ, the Spirit of the Lord, the Spirit of Jesus. Paul thought of the Spirit not simply as a force, or power making intermittent appearances, but as the abiding principle of the Christian life, the possession of which provides the means for overcoming the power of sin and attaining the promise of redemption (Rom. 8:1-2 and 9-16). Paul personifies the Spirit, thinking of it as the power of God now identified with the activity and continuing influence of Jesus (Rom. 8:26).

With the departure of Jesus from the earth, teachings concerning the Spirit took on new and added significance for the early church. It is in this context that Acts deals with this important theme. The Holy Spirit is the continuer of Jesus' work.

Pentecost. The apostles attributed their transformation of life and outlook to the gift and activity of the Holy Spirit. Before his ascension Jesus had promised them that "you shall receive power when the Holy Spirit has come upon you; and you shall be my witnesses in Jerusalem and in all Judea and Samaria and to the end of the earth" (1:8). Thus, even though Jesus was no longer on earth in the flesh, his presence might be known, his power experienced, and his work carried on through the agency of the Holy Spirit. The apostles were not to be left alone.

The account in Acts of the coming of the Holy Spirit at Pentecost is indeed dramatic:

> When the day of Pentecost had come, they were all together in one place. And suddenly a sound came from heaven like the rush of a mighty wind, and it filled all the house where they were sitting. And there appeared to them tongues as of fire, distributed and resting on each one of them. And they were all filled with the Holy Spirit and began to speak in other tongues, as the Spirit gave them utterance.
>
> Acts 2:1-4

Actually there are two versions as to when and how the Holy Spirit first came upon the apostles. According to John 20:22 it was on the day of the Resurrection that Jesus breathed upon the disciples, saying, "Receive the Holy Spirit." According to Acts the Spirit descended fifty days after the Resurrection.

There are several features of the Acts account which are of special interest. The gift of the Spirit is said to have taken place on Pentecost. Pentecost, according to Jewish custom, involved a celebration on the fiftieth day after a seven-week period for the reaping of barley and wheat (see Deut. 16:9 and Lev. 23:15-16). Many years later the gift of God's law to Moses at Sinai was also celebrated at Pentecost, thus uniting in one festival the people's thanks for the gift of food with their gratitude for the divine blessing of spiritual revelation. It was appropriate, to the first Jewish Christians, that the gift of the Holy Spirit should be granted fifty days after the Resurrection, thus becoming the Christian Pentecost. References to wind and fire recall earlier biblical symbols of the presence of God. Thus, the promise set forth in Luke 3:16 of baptism "with the Holy Spirit and with fire" is fulfilled. The reference to "tongues as of fire" may well be related to the speaking in tongues referred to later.

Whereas "speaking in tongues" (*glossolalia*) was a not uncommon phenomenon in Christian circles where ecstatic feeling and behavior was prized, the Acts account is distinctive in saying that the apostles spoke in varied languages. Men from "every nation under heaven" heard the apostles speaking in their languages. This is quite different from Paul's comment on one who speaks in a tongue: "No one understands him . . ." (I Cor. 14:2).

Peter's sermon at Pentecost (2:14-40) claims the coming of the Spirit that day to be the fulfillment of Joel's prophecy. Thus, the last days are at hand. The key theological ideas of the Book of Acts are set forth in this sermon. The pouring out of the Spirit by the ascended Jesus shows him to be "Lord and Christ" (2:36). Thus, the presence of the Holy Spirit (in the church) is used to prove the truth of a doctrine or belief concerning Jesus.

According to Acts the coming of the Holy Spirit at Pentecost inaugurates a new age—the age of the Spirit. It marks the beginning of the church's mission "to the end of the earth."

Concerning the Holy Spirit. The gift of the Holy Spirit, according to Acts, is not limited to those who were present on Pentecost.

> "For the promise is to you and to your children and to all that are far off, every one whom the Lord our God calls to him."
>
> Acts 2:39

As the story unfolds there are reports of many persons receiving the gift of the Holy Spirit as they responded in faith to the preaching of the Christian message. The church is the home of the Spirit. The Spirit is represented in Acts as working with varying degrees of power in different persons. Peter, Paul, Barnabas, and the Seven, including Stephen, are all described as being possessed by the Holy Spirit in particularly remarkable ways. The Pentecost account refers, of course, to the receiving of the Spirit on the part of the Jewish group in Jerusalem. A similar experience is reported in reference to a Gentile Christian group in Acts 10:44-48; 11:15; 15:8.

The connection between the reception of the Holy Spirit and baptism and the laying on of hands is not entirely clear in Acts. In Peter's Pentecost sermon (2:38) the gift of the Spirit is definitely related to repentance and baptism:

> "Repent, and be baptized every one of you in the name of Jesus Christ for the forgiveness of your sins; and you shall receive the gift of the Holy Spirit."

In the case of Cornelius and his household, however, baptism *followed* the reception of the Spirit (10:44-48). The coming of the Holy Spirit upon the Samaritan converts baptized by Philip was delayed until Peter and John arrived from Jerusalem and laid their hands upon the new converts (8:12-17). In the case of Paul it is not entirely clear whether the gift of the Holy Spirit attended the laying on of hands by Ananias or whether the author intended to associate the gift of the Spirit with baptism (9:17-18). Apollos is said to have been "fervent in spirit" speaking and teaching accurately concerning Jesus even though he "knew only the baptism of John" (18:25). Thus, there is no consistent pattern in Acts in so far as the relationship of the gift of the Holy Spirit to baptism and the laying on of hands is concerned. Usually, however, baptism and the gift of the Spirit are associated.

If the author of Acts had been a theologian he probably would have been more precise in spelling out the relationship of the Holy Spirit to God and to Jesus Christ. It is frequently assumed that the author intended to identify the Holy Spirit with the Risen Christ. Even though Jesus was no longer present on earth in the body, he was present with the apostles and other Christians in the Spirit. In Acts 16:7 the Holy Spirit is referred to as "the Spirit of Jesus." This approach would seem to be harmonious with the Fourth Gospel where Jesus is portrayed appearing to the disciples on the day of Resurrection: ". . . he breathed on them, and said to them, 'Receive the Holy Spirit . . .'" (John 20:22). Presumably it was truly the Spirit of Jesus which was given.

In Acts the situation is not quite so clear. Jesus is described as ascending to heaven, "being exalted at the right hand of God," receiving from the Father the promise of the Holy Spirit, and pouring out the Spirit of God upon his followers. In Acts the Holy Spirit is to be understood in theological terms and is closely associated with God and in function is virtually identical. The more technical discussions pertaining to the relationships of God, Jesus Christ, and the Holy Spirit did not come until some years after the Book of Acts was written. However, it is clear that the author of Acts wished to convey the message that the Holy Spirit was the manifestation of God's presence and activity in the world and especially in Christian history; furthermore, the Holy Spirit was the vital link between the ascended Jesus and those on earth called to continue his work and carry forth his mission.

The Work of the Spirit. Since the author of Acts puts such great emphasis on the Holy Spirit, it is essential that we examine what, in his opinion, is its particular function.

Within all that is said in Acts on this subject lies the conviction that the Holy Spirit provides the motivation and the enabling power for the early church to go forth in mission. The Holy Spirit provides the dynamic required to carry on the mission of Jesus in the world (1:8). It accounts for the boldness of the apostles and the power of their gospel message, as well as the amazing success of the Christian movement.

More immediately the Holy Spirit was thought to inspire on occasion the speaking in tongues, the power to prophesy, and the power to work miracles. As has already been indicated, the incident of speaking in tongues at Pentecost was said to be a speaking in foreign languages. In this sense, intentionally or unintentionally, we have a divergence from the uttering of inarticulate sounds which has frequently been associated with religious meetings of a highly emotional nature. We recall that Paul was much concerned about some of the speaking in tongues he observed in the churches. He wrote at length to the Christians at Corinth on this matter (TEXT, p. 24). He recognized that such speaking in tongues may fail to edify, and actually lead to disorder in the churches. He endeavored to direct this sort of activity into ethical channels, bringing it under the control of reason (I Cor. 12:6-11 and 13-14). In Galatians he described the "fruit of the Spirit" as "love, joy, peace, patience, kindness, goodness, faithfulness, gentleness, self-control" (5:22).

Acts says little about the ethical implications of the work of the Holy Spirit. It is in relation to *the mission of the church* that we find the deeper significance of the Holy Spirit in Acts. The Christian mission is God's mission—and, through the Holy Spirit, God provides the power necessary for the carrying on of that mission. Thus, the Holy Spirit *enables* Peter and John to speak in boldness (4:31); *directs* Peter (10:19-20); *predicts* famine (11:28); *instructs* the church at Antioch to set aside Barnabas and Saul for special work (13:2); *sends* them *forth* (13:4); *enables* Saul to confront Elymas, the magician (13:8-12); *forbids* the speaking of the word in Asia and Bithynia (16:

6-7); *informs* Paul that bonds and afflictions await him (20:23); *designates guardians* of the flock (20: 28); *warns* Paul (21:4).

The Christian movement as seen in Acts is dynamic, inspired, outreaching, and triumphant. Its zeal, its astonishing success, and its growth are due to the presence and working of the Holy Spirit. It is no wonder that for many centuries the Christian church has turned to Acts for a better understanding of its own beginnings and, also, for a clearer understanding of the spiritual power which animated its earliest leaders and converts.

THE HOLY SPIRIT IN THE LIFE OF TODAY

Many persons in our day are completely bewildered by discussions pertaining to the Holy Spirit. The language of "the Spirit" suggests to them the image of ghosts or fiery tongues or persons in some strange ecstatic state—all of which may seem quite irrelevant in our own time. Yet, these same persons may be sincerely seeking for a deeper religious life of their own, a deepened sense of God's presence and power in their lives. It is important that we not permit language or particular thought-forms of earlier times to get in the way of spiritual realities. With this in mind, let us seek a deepened understanding of the underlying meaning of the Holy Spirit in our own lives and time. Is there—for us—a *new life* in the Spirit?

The Experience Behind the Doctrine. All profound experiences of life elude adequate expression in words.

A moving experience of beauty, the excitement which attends a new discovery of important truth, a transforming experience of love, all defy adequate expression in words. So it is in the life of religion. The deepest experiences of God cannot fully be put into words; yet we are constrained to bear some witness to them. Thus, religion frequently employs non-literal language—the language of symbolism, poetry, music, drama. The stories of Moses in the presence of the burning bush (Exod. 3:1-12), Isaiah in the Temple (Isa., chapter 6), the apostles at Pentecost (Acts, chapter 2), all suggest experiences of deep inner spiritual significance.

When we turn to theology we encounter time-honored words, phrases, and doctrines. These all have their place, but they should never be permitted to become ends in themselves. At best, they are tools or instruments used to try to give expression to the realities of the Christian life. So it is in discussions of the Holy Spirit. Back of the words is experience. It is for us to try to find out more about the experience and then seek its meaning for our own lives.

The author of Acts portrayed the early Christian movement as being Spirit-directed and infused-directed. He portrayed the leaders of that movement and the Christian community as being Spirit-filled, Spirit-motivated. Was there, indeed, something profoundly important in the experience of the early church which we would do well to seek in our own lives?

It appears that back of the various New Testament teachings concerning the Holy Spirit there were three types of related experience: first, *the experience of a changed life;* second, *the experience of enabling, comforting, directing power;* third, *the experience of courage and will to witness.* As indicated above, the Book of Acts portrays in striking ways the changes that were experienced in the lives of certain early Christians. Likewise, the author speaks of the new dynamic which was released in and through the Christian movement. Finally, his major theme is the missionary outreach of the early church—empowered and directed by the Spirit of God. In speaking of these matters he naturally used language and thought-forms appropriate to his own time, some of which may be confusing to us today. The question is, was he speaking of matters which are important in the life of our time?

The Reality of New Life. Many centuries ago the author of the Book of Job wrote (5:4, 6-7):

> "His sons are far from safety,
>   they are crushed in the gate,
>   and there is no one to deliver them. . . .
> For affliction does not come from the dust,
>   nor does trouble sprout from the ground;
> but man is born to trouble
>   as the sparks fly upward."

There is, indeed, a built-in hardness to human life. Under these circumstances, all normal persons seek courage, meaning, and wholeness in their lives. Man is both sustained and threatened by the world around him. His own nature is also complex and he is frequently a problem to himself. Man has capacities for both destruction and creation. Thus, man's experience is that of a suffering, sinning, and aspiring creature. He is involved in both good and evil.

People meet with varying degrees of success in their search for courage, meaning, and wholeness. For some persons, life seems to be a meaningless burden; for some, it is an endless round of duties adding up to no particular significance; but for others, it is fraught with profound purpose and possibility. The Christian life is a life lived in the light of the living God whose presence in our world and experience makes all things new. It is a life of purpose and power— reflecting love of God and neighbor.

It has been said that the best argument for Christianity is a Christian. Indeed, it is in the lives of persons who exemplify the great teachings of Christian faith that we may find assurance that there *is* a new life of faith, hope, and love. We all know persons whose lives bear witness to the reality of God in human experience. Through them we know that there is "a more excellent way" toward which we may all aspire.

One of the values of reading significant biography is the mounting evidence we find there that human life can be significant. And one of the values of reading such a work as the Book of Acts is its testimony to a new life truly worth living. Indeed, the Book of Acts confronts each of us with the questions:

Is there the possibility of a changed life for *me*?
Is there the possibility of new power in *my* life?
Is there the possibility of a new motivation for going into the world as a living witness to the living God?

We can study the Book of Acts simply as an interesting historical document, or we can go on from there and ask whether it speaks to us in any vital way. If we follow the second course, we may find ourselves confronting some of the central issues of our own lives.

Century after century the Christian church proclaims the good news that indeed there is the promise and possibility of a new life. God is a living God who through Jesus Christ makes possible new beginnings and victory of the spirit over the most devastating events in human experience. Out of an old existence marked by suffering, death, sin, there can and does emerge a new life of faith, hope, and love. The most difficult problems we face are not always removed, but they are understood in a new light. What before seemed meaningless is now seen in the light of God's reality which gives to all things a changed meaning.

It is the primary purpose of the church to communicate this good news and to bear witness to its reality. Behind all the organizational activities in which we become involved is the promise of new life and new hope. Acts refers in several places to the Christian movement as "The Way" (9:2; 19:9 and 23; 24:14). The church of our own time is called to bear witness to "a more excellent way"—of faith, hope, and love.

A Theological Understanding of the New Life. Once we are confronted by evidence that (1) lives *can* be changed (transformed) to deeper levels of faith, hope, and love; (2) human beings *can* experience enabling, comforting, directing power; (3) persons *can* be motivated to new lives of witness and service—the question emerges as to how all this can be. It is one of the tasks of theology to show how God is present and effects these transformations in human lives.

The doctrine of the Holy Spirit affirms that God is indeed active and present in the world and in the lives and relationships of human beings. The doctrine of the Holy Spirit is a denial of the view that God is far removed from the world and man—indifferent to his concerns. God as Holy Spirit refers to the presence of God with us and in us. A familiar affirmation of faith refers to the Holy Spirit as "the Divine Presence in our lives, whereby we are kept in perpetual remembrance of the truth of Christ, and find strength and help in time of need." [1]

The doctrine of the Trinity teaches that God is one, but that he reveals himself in three roles: as creator, sustainer, and law-giver (Father); as redeemer (Son); as life-giving presence and power (Holy Spirit). There is no developed doctrine of the Trinity in the Bible (this came later in Christian history). But we do find materials for it in the Scripture. The doctrine of the Trinity endeavors to hold together the various roles or functions of God, insisting that the God known as creator is the same God experienced in Jesus Christ and the same God experienced in the coming of new life and power. When we sing "God in three persons, blessed Trinity," the reference is not to three separate personalities, as one might suppose. Rather the term *persona* means "mask" and suggests the idea of an actor wearing different masks in different scenes, enacting different roles, although always the same actor. So God, although one, is creator, redeemer, and life-giving Spirit.

---

[1] *The Methodist Hymnal*, page 512.

34

While the author of Acts lived before the doctrine of the Trinity had been formulated, he obviously believed that the God who created the world and in whom "we live and move and have our being," and who raised Jesus from the dead, making him both Lord and Christ, was the same God who comforted, empowered, and directed the early Christians through his Spirit. It was his way of saying that God continued to be available to man in a saving way. The Holy Spirit was operative in the making of new persons and in the impartation of unusual gifts and powers.

Our Wesleyan Heritage. John Wesley had much to say about the Holy Spirit in the life of man. He associated the Spirit of God with creation and providence. He saw the Spirit's operation in the granting of responsible freedom and moral conscience to man. If the work of Jesus Christ was fundamental in man's coming to a new, forgiven relationship of acceptance with God (justification), the Holy Spirit was operative in man's turning to God in conversion, in the gift of inner assurance, and in man's growth in grace (sanctification and perfection). Thus, Wesley placed much emphasis upon the work of the Holy Spirit in the Christian life.

John Wesley was a preacher concerned with the salvation of men. He spoke much of theology and doctrine, but almost invariably in relationship to the Christian life. His was a message of Christian experience. He regarded the Bible as his supreme authority in theological matters, but his hope was that biblical truths would be confirmed in the personal experience of his listeners. He was convinced that God moves in the minds and hearts and wills of men in a transforming way—and this, to him, was evidence of the work of the Spirit.

Some theologies have stressed the idea of forgiveness and acceptance to the neglect of actual growth in the Christian life. John Wesley sought to combine both ideas in his preaching. He taught that we are justified in faith and perfected in love. The work of the Holy Spirit is basic in the perfecting processes— enabling man to live a life of love. Wesley acknowledged that the Holy Spirit operates in somewhat different ways in individuals of varying personalities and temperaments.

Wesley believed that doctrine or form without Spirit was dead. Fearful that the Methodists might lose the vitality which marks the presence of the Spirit, he wrote:

> I am not afraid that the people called Methodists should ever cease to exist, either in Europe or America. But I am afraid, lest they should only exist as a dead sect, having the form of religion without the power.[1]

Whereas he believed that no one could manipulate the Holy Spirit, Wesley did believe that the life of the Spirit was associated with the life of repentance, sound doctrine, attendance upon the various ordinances of God (including the preaching of the Word and the administration of the Sacraments), and obedience to various disciplines of the Christian life. He called his followers to faithfulness in these matters.

---

[1] Luke Tyerman, *The Life and Times of the Reverend John Wesley* (New York: Harper & Bros., 1870), Vol. III, p. 519.

Historically, Methodism has tended to subordinate doctrine to life. To know God as a saving God, to be able to testify to the redeeming work of Jesus Christ in one's own life, and to give evidence of the work of the Holy Spirit in an ever-growing and deepening life of love has seemed to be the most important thing to Methodists. Considerable variation in thought and interpretation of doctrine has been permitted so long as there is evidence of *new life* in the Spirit. For this reason Methodism has not been plagued by numerous heresy trials and demand for conformity of thought. Rather, it has emphasized a religion of the Spirit.

A Religion of the Spirit in the Space Age. What does it mean for us to take the doctrine of the Holy Spirit seriously in our own time? Very simply, it means to take seriously the belief that the same God who in times past has been made known in creation, in the fundamental structures and processes of life, in the call to justice and mercy proclaimed by the prophets, in the wisdom vouchsafed to sincere seekers after truth, in lives of dedicated service, and supremely in the self-giving love manifest in Jesus Christ—this same God is present and active in our world today, offering men a new life of faith and hope and love.

One of the great dangers of religion is that it become static and uncreative, content to rest at ease in what has been said and done in the past. The doctrine of the Holy Spirit reminds us that God is a living God, whose revelations are unending, present with us in our immediate situations, ever seeking to dispel ignorance and error, leading us into new truth and new life. The doctrine of the Holy Spirit reminds us that, although life may not be easy, there is power to match our problems, and the Spirit is there challenging us to accept the call of our possibilities. The doctrine of the Holy Spirit reminds us that God is a contemporary God—and we are called to seek his will and way in our own lives. This is a message desperately needed in our time. It is a message which helps us understand that religion can be dynamic and relevant in our lives today.

The Spirit of the living God does not come to those who would evade or run away from life's responsibilities. Rather, it is granted to those who feel a sense of need and also a sense of responsibility. The Spirit comes to those who are open to new truth and new guidance, who are faithful in the disciplines of the inner life, who seek to come to grips with the real problems of life and to make a contribution to their solutions. To these persons the Spirit of God is made manifest. Such men venture forth in the faith that God is at the heart of life calling each one, personally, to take a responsible part in the world.

They do not walk alone. God is at hand. God is present to transform life, to hold out the possibility of new beginnings, to empower, comfort, and guide, to send forth his human creatures in lives of glad and grateful service and witness.

Behind the ancient stories of the gift of the Holy Spirit there is the transforming experience of God's life in the souls of men. That experience can be ours today. We, too, can know *new life* in the Spirit.

THREE:

the church as fellowship and institution

THE BOOK OF ACTS HAS LONG BEEN REGARDED AS a major source of information concerning the early church. The major reason for the writing of Acts was probably apologetic [defensive, see TEXT, p. 7] rather than historical; nevertheless, Acts throws much light on the early church and raises some issues exceedingly important for consideration in our own time as we think of the church and its mission.

It may well be that this study of the early church and the church today will lead us to discover underlying truths about early Christianity which will help us to achieve a deepened understanding of the church and its needs and its purposes in our own day.

THE CHURCH IN ACTS: FELLOWSHIP

A number of terms are used in Acts to indicate followers of Jesus Christ: believers, disciples, Christians. It is interesting to note that although the term "disciples" is used many times, the word "Christian" appears only once (26:28) and the word "Christians" appears only once (11:26). A number of references are made to "the Way" so that disciples might be thought of as "those of the Way."

When we come to references pertaining to the disciples or Christians or believers or those of the Way in their association, or *communal* life, there are two terms used in Acts of special importance: *ecclesia* (translated "church") and *koinonia* (translated "fellowship"). The term *ecclesia* is used in Acts in a number of instances; the term *koinonia* appears only once (although it is found eighteen times in the New Testament, thirteen of these instances being in the writings of Paul). Both because of their place in Acts, and because of their frequent usage in contemporary discussion of the church, it is well for us to examine these terms more carefully.

Ecclesia. The Greek word *ecclesia*, meaning a meeting or gathering, does not necessarily have religious connotations, but in many instances it does. In the translation of the Old Testament from Hebrew into Greek the term *ecclesia* is frequently used for the Hebrew *qâhâl*. The term *qâhâl* in the Old Testament applies to people coming or meeting together for any purpose—good or evil.

In the New Testament the term *ecclesia* acquires religious associations. It is used to signify a gathering for some particular religious purpose; a company called into being by God through Christ; a chosen people—the renewed Israel; the body of Christ; or the people of God. There are many ways of expressing the *ecclesia* or church idea in the New Testament.

Although in Acts we do not find a developed theory or doctrine of the church, we do find numerous references to the *ecclesia* or church.

The second chapter of Acts implies that the church came into being at Pentecost with the gift of the Holy Spirit. Indeed, insofar as we have a general theory of the church in Acts, it is that the church is *the company of those who have received the gift of the Holy Spirit* (10:47; 11:15-18).

Acts suggests that the church includes those who have responded in belief, repentance, and faith to God's work in Jesus Christ. The role of man's belief, inspired by the Spirit, is important. However, it is the divine initiative in calling the church into being and then sustaining, guiding, inspiring, and empowering it through the Holy Spirit which is particularly stressed. The church is of God; it is God's instrumentality; it lives by virtue of the divine presence and activity within its life.

Another major theme of Acts is that *the Christian movement is the true Judaism.* The author points out the faithfulness of the first Christians to synagogue and temple services; their reverence for Scripture; their superior understanding of the true meaning of Scripture. According to this view the Jews, by their rejection of Jesus, have forfeited their distinctive role as the chosen people of God, and the Christian movement is now the "new Israel." The church is to be understood in this "called" relationship to God—"called" to witness to his saving work in Jesus Christ. It is therefore the contention of the author of Acts that the recognition and privileges accorded Judaism under Roman law ought now to be transferred to Christianity.

Thus, we see that the *ecclesia*, or church, of the Book of Acts is much more than simply a meeting or gathering. It is a meeting or gathering *inspired of God*, empowered and directed by the Holy Spirit, called to carry on the work of God in the world until the return of Jesus. This return was expected to be in the near future.

Koinonia. In Acts 2:42 we are told that, "They devoted themselves to the apostles' teaching and fellowship, to the breaking of bread and the prayers." The word "fellowship" is here a translation of the Greek word *koinonia*, a word which carries a meaning of great importance for later discussions of the church.

The word *koinonia* suggests "having something in common, an association, communion, fellowship, close relationship." Paul frequently used the word in his letters to convey the idea of fellowship with Jesus Christ (I Cor. 1:9); a close relationship with the gospel (Phil. 1:5); a close relationship to the poor (Rom. 15:26); a fellow-feeling (II Cor. 9:13); or the participation in something (Philemon 6). In Acts the reference is clearly to fellowship and (or) brotherly unity. The church or Christian community is addressed as "brothers" in at least thirty places in this book (1:15-16; 2:29; 3:17).

One of the interesting features of Acts is its author's obvious concern to impress his potential readers with the unity and inner harmony of the Christian groups. If, as has been suggested, a basic purpose of the author was *to address Roman officials in a conciliatory way*, it is understandable that he would seek to present this picture of the church. If we turn to some of Paul's letters (for example, Gal. 2:11-21), we have evidence of conflict and of internal differences. This does not mean that the author of Acts was endeavoring to distort the facts, but rather that he sought to emphasize one aspect of the church's fellowship. He does indeed report the contention between Paul and Barnabas (15:36-40) and the debate within the church over the issue of circumcision (15:1-2). In the main, however, the picture of the church in Acts is that of a fellowship living in harmony and unity of purpose:

> Now the company of those who believed were of one heart and soul. . . .
>
> Acts 4:32

Fellowship in Teaching, Breaking of Bread, and Prayer. Meetings of the early Christians, it seems, took place frequently, perhaps daily. Christians in Jerusalem gathered at the temple or in their homes; they also attended the synagogues. Acts gives us no picture of a uniform procedure but does report that "they devoted themselves to the apostles' teaching and fellowship, to the breaking of bread and the prayers" (2:42).

At the time Acts was written, the Christians had no separate places for public worship. They participated in temple and synagogue services. However, their attention to "the prayers" was not limited to temple and synagogue. Family worship and prayers in homes undoubtedly formed an important part of the life of the early Christians.

It is to be assumed that attention to the apostles' teaching involved a Messianic interpretation of the Old Testament together with the words and deeds of Jesus. We are told, "And every day in the temple and at home they did not cease teaching and preaching Jesus as the Christ" (5:42). It is interesting that nothing is said in Acts concerning any teaching carried on prior to the conversion to Christianity, nor concerning the private life or ethical standards of the Christian. The teaching which is stressed in Acts has to do with the proclamation of Jesus as the Christ.

Whether or not the "breaking of bread" refers to an ordinary meal or whether it had particular religious significance in Acts we cannot be certain. In 2:46 the breaking of bread and the partaking of food are mentioned together (also see 20:7-11; 27:35). It may well be that the breaking of bread symbolized a bond of fellowship as well as a means of support of the needy.

A Fellowship of the Concerned. Two references in Acts speak of the Christians as having all things in common (2:44 and 4:32). Precisely what this entailed or how long this arrangement persisted we do not know. However, *the idea of sharing and helping those in need is a persistent theme in Acts.* Since the return of Jesus was expected in the near future, it is quite understandable that members of this waiting fellowship would hold things in common.

The picture presented us is that of a fellowship of

the concerned. Real estate was sold and the proceeds given to the apostles for distribution among the needy (4:34 through 5:11; 2:44-45). Special arrangements were made and responsibilities assigned for distributing goods to widows (6:1). The concern of the Christians of Antioch for those in need in Judea during the famine in the days of Claudius (A.D. 41-54) is reported in Acts 11:27-30.

The primary purpose of the Book of Acts, however, is not to describe the internal life of the early church. It is much more concerned with showing how the mission of the Christian community is God-inspired and God-directed. However, sufficient material is presented to indicate the internal concern and mutual care which existed. In all is the underlying theme of the church as the fellowship of those who are changed persons, having received the gift of the Holy Spirit.

An Inclusive Fellowship. Perhaps the greatest crisis that confronted the Christian movement in the first century centered around the issue as to whether the church was to be a truly inclusive fellowship or was to remain a party or "sect" within Judaism. Upon the determination of this issue rested the future of Christianity—whether it was to become a universal religion or remain a part of Judaism.

The original Christian group was exclusively Jewish. Its members continued to participate in temple and synagogue services, regarding Jesus as the long-awaited Messiah or Christ. The ethical teachings of Jesus were looked upon as a new Torah or Law. This is the general point of view reflected in the Gospel of Matthew, written by a Jewish Christian for Jewish Christians and for Jews who might become converts: Christianity is interpreted as a higher Judaism.

New problems inevitably arose as Christianity moved into the Gentile world. Of special importance was the question as to whether Gentiles desiring to become Christians were to be subject to the Jewish rite of circumcision. There were those who said, "Unless you are circumcised according to the custom of Moses, you cannot be saved" (15:1). Some Gentiles were willing to be initiated into Judaism by this rite, but others refused. Those Gentiles who were attracted to Christianity and who participated in synagogue life, but who refused circumcision as a Jewish rite, were called "God Fearers," a term which distinguished them from "proselytes," circumcised Gentile believers. Of these uncircumcised there was an increasing number.

It is quite understandable that Paul should be the person to stand forthrightly for Christianity as a universal religion (Gal. 3:28; Col. 3:11), unfettered by the demands of ritualistic Judaism. He himself had once been a Pharisee, a Jew of the strictest sort, holding to the absolute claims of the Law. But, after his encounter with Christ on the road to Damascus, he had come to a radically different point of view. Increasingly frustrated in his own inner life by the demands of the Law (Rom. 7:1-25), Paul had found in Jesus Christ a new allegiance and a new life. Released from the demands of the old Law, he was now subject to the new and emancipating law and Spirit of Christ. His was an *inner* discipline and law and power. Whereas in the past he was enslaved, he was now free—subject only to the lordship of Jesus Christ. Under these circumstances he was not one to insist on the Jewish initiatory rite of circumcision; for him baptism into Christ superseded the old law. In Galatians, chapters 2 and 3, we read Paul's own account of his controversy with Peter and James and others over this matter.

The Book of Acts, with its strong emphasis on the universal nature of Christianity, makes much of this issue, showing how early Christianity broke through the limitations of ritualistic Judaism and became an inclusive fellowship. It contains accounts of divinely approved Gentile conversions, of Peter's testimony concerning the Holy Spirit coming to the Gentiles (11:1-18), and of the conference in Jerusalem wherein Peter, Barnabas, and Paul all spoke concerning God's work among the Gentiles. Out of this conference there came agreement on a basic issue—circumcision would not be required of Gentile Christians as long as certain other disciplines were observed. The way was cleared for an ongoing mission to the Gentiles (15:1-35). Thus, out of the experience and consultation of the early church there emerged the conviction that the gospel was for all men. Henceforth, membership in the church was not to be limited on the basis of nationality or race; qualifications for membership were spiritual in nature. The Christian church was now seen as truly an inclusive fellowship —the company of those who had responded to God's saving work in Christ in repentance and faith, and who were now guided by the Holy Spirit.

Since the early church lived in the expectation of Jesus' return in the near future, it was a waiting community. This being the case, there was no need for elaborate organization. This is precisely the situation reflected in the Book of Acts. The Christian church as a highly organized institution was unknown. A new movement, guided by the Spirit, waiting for the return of Jesus, required a minimum of officials and organization. However, responsibilities for carrying out various tasks were recognized and sometimes assigned. In these matters each local church was virtually autonomous—independent in its government and organization.

The apostles, of course, held a position of special respect and authority. This group included those who had known Jesus and had worked with him during his earthly ministry. Their names, minus that of Judas, are listed in Acts 1:13-26. These were the original disciples. Matthias was selected to replace Judas. To this group was added Paul who vigorously argued his claim to his apostleship in letters to both the Galatians and Corinthians (Gal. 1:1, 11; and I Cor. 9:2; 15:8-10). James, the brother of Jesus, came to a position of leadership in the church at Jerusalem and may appropriately be considered as one of the apostles; Barnabas is also usually numbered among them. The apostles held a unique status in the early church. In Acts 6:4 the distinctive ministry of the apostles is described as "prayer and the ministry of the word." However, it is clear that many matters of a policy-making and administrative character were handled by the apostles—in Jerusalem and in other communities.

Prophets and teachers also held distinctive places of leadership in the church. We are told that the prophets "exhorted the brethren," but it appears that they were further concerned with prophesying, sometimes accompanied by speaking in tongues (19:6); but Paul was deeply concerned that speaking in tongues should be brought under the control of reason and love (TEXT, p. 28). The teachers referred to in Acts presumably devoted themselves to instruction and the interpretation of the apostolic message. The varied ministries in the church were all regarded as being the direct gift of the Spirit (I Cor. 12:1-11, 27-31).

Elders or presbyters were persons who early came to positions of leadership in the churches. They may well have been senior members of the Christian communities who were held in high respect. The first reference to the appointment of elders as officials of the church is noted in Acts 14:23. No reference is made to bishops in Acts. An elder frequently functioned somewhat like a pastor in a local congregation. In some instances a board of elders was formed.

In the opening verses of the sixth chapter of Acts we find an interesting account of the special assignment of a particular responsibility. The Hellenistic or Greek-speaking Jews complained that some of the needy among them were being neglected in the distribution of relief. To meet this need, seven men "of good repute, full of the Spirit and of wisdom" were selected by popular choice "to serve tables." This was done to relieve the apostles of duties other than the preaching of the word of God. Among those selected to form the group of seven were Philip, who encountered the Ethiopian eunuch, and Stephen, the first Christian martyr. This group was approved by the apostles who "prayed and laid their hands upon them." It is sometimes said that in the naming of this group of seven we have the establishment of the *diaconate* (deacons) in the church; however, the word deacon is not used in Acts.

Thus, we see that the organization of the early church, as described in Acts, was *simple*. Furthermore, it was *functional*—designed to meet specific and contemporary needs. That the rank and file of the church had a voice in some decision-making is suggested in Acts 6:5 and 15:22.

THE CHURCH IN OUR TIME

Having considered the fellowship and organization of the early church as it is pictured in Acts, let us now ask what we may learn from this in our own time. How is the church different from any other fellowship or organization? What is the deeper meaning and purpose of our life together in the church? By what norm or standards ought we to be judging our churches? These are questions of the greatest importance. Can the Book of Acts help us as we search for answers to these and related questions?

It is obvious that we are separated from the early church by many centuries in point of time. The world has changed greatly and the circumstances and culture in which we now live differ in many ways from those which existed in the first century. For instance, the church was just getting started then; it has now been long in existence and has become an established institution. Thus, it would be unrealistic to suppose that we could *return* to the conditions which prevailed in the early church, and equally unrealistic for us to try to copy the early church in all of its ways. We are told that the Holy Spirit will lead us into new truth, sometimes breaking through old structures that we may come into a larger life and fuller understanding. We need to learn from the past without being enslaved by it.

Thus, we turn to the Book of Acts for what it has to teach us about the early church, providing insight into what the church has been and what it might be. From this study we must go on to seek a deeper understanding of what the church is called to be in our own time. Just as the early Christians, in fellowship with God and each other in the Spirit, were called to deal with issues of their own time, so we today are called to face current opportunities and problems. In this understanding, let us phrase our questions as follows: *What* is the church? *Who* is the church? *Where* is the church? Acts has insight and inspiration on these.

What Is the Church? In the light of our study we may reply that *the church is both fellowship and insituation.* It is *ecclesia,* a people gathered together, but it is more. It is *koinonia,* a fellowship participating together in something profoundly important, exhibiting brotherly unity.

People are brought and held together by numerous binding elements: a common need, a common fate, a common failure, fear, or hostility, a common history, a common love or loyalty, a common hope. And sometimes people come together simply because they cannot bear being alone. Christian fellowship involves a number of the factors just mentioned, but its central binding, motivating, inspiring power is the living Spirit of God, keeping us in perpetual remembrance of the truth of Christ and leading us forth into new and higher levels of that life which is intended for God's human creatures.

Some years ago while driving to a church meeting I was delayed by a minor automobile accident which occurred a short distance ahead. In a matter of moments a crowd of onlookers assembled, but in a very few minutes the crowd dispersed again. There was nothing of abiding interest or concern to hold it together. Shortly thereafter I found myself a part of a Christian fellowship wrestling with some of the great issues of faith. Here was true *koinonia*—and how different it was from the crowd which had gathered and dispersed so quickly! Depth, direction, and continuity exist in Christian fellowship because of its binding Center and Head, and because of the shared hopes and aspirations he inspires.

The fellowship of the church is fellowship with God and other Christians. It is impossible to be a Christian "in isolation" with no sense of belonging. We may be separated from one another in space and time, but Christian fellowship spans space and time; there is a "fellowship of kindred minds," created, sustained, and inspired by the Spirit of the living God. To be a Christian is to participate in this fellowship.

The Christian fellowship gathers together those who have responded and are responding in faith and hope and love to God's work in creation and redemption—supremely to the love manifest in Jesus Christ. It is a fellowship of those whose minds have been illumined with new understanding, whose hearts have been filled with a deeper trust and love, whose purposes have found new depth and direction in the will of God and the mind of Christ. It is a fellowship of those who are growing "to mature manhood, to the measure of the stature of the fulness of Christ."

Authentic Christian fellowship is inclusive, cutting across lines of nation, race, education, and economic status. It permits diversity within its underlying unity. The authentic Christian church incarnates in its own life the healing, reconciling, life-giving Spirit of Christ. The church is called to be a group agency of revelation and mediation—revealing the living God in its own life, and mediating to needy persons the healing grace of Christ's own Spirit.

As a growing boy I lived for some years in a small Minnesota community. Whenever there was a death in the community the village bell tolled. Thus, everyone knew that death had come and a member of our community had passed on. There was a solemnity about it, a dignity, and an intimacy. But now sometimes, living in a large city, I may see a funeral procession pass and scarcely pause to wonder who has died. Then sometimes I remember the tolling of the village bell.

Our world has changed, and we are changing, too. But how much we need true depth in the fellowships of our contemporary world! How much we need a continuing fellowship in which the great experiences of life are recognized, celebrated, dedicated, and shared in the context of Christian faith! How much we need communities of concern and mutuality in which we know and are known! How much we need the creating, redeeming, life-giving fellowship which is the church!

However much the church is fellowship, it is also institution. But the organizational, institutional aspects of the church's life are not ends in themselves. They are means to the church's life as a ministering fellowship, enabling our mission today to continue and to be effective. Whenever the organizational phase of the church comes to take first place, whenever it hinders rather than helps the underlying religious spirit and purpose of the church, "The Way" has been missed.

However, just as danger exists in overemphasizing the importance of the organizational phase of the church's life, so there is the danger of defining the church exclusively in spiritual terms so that responsibility for discipline and for carrying on the practical concerns of the church is neglected. It is also true that we may be deceived into thinking that external, numerical success is the measure of spiritual growth in the church. On the other hand, we need the organizational feature of the church's life if we are to have a continuing ministry of depth. The church is both fellowship and institution.

We have observed that in the early church organization was simple and functional. By necessity our organization is more complex today. However, we would do well to apply the functional test. Do our various offices exist to serve a purpose and meet a real need? Are we prepared to make such changes as are indicated by new situations and new needs? We are called to serve in the living present—and that demands a continuing re-examination of our "church machinery" in the light of the needs and responsibilities as they currently arise.

Throughout its history Methodism has endeavored to steer a middle course between the concepts of the church as fellowship and as institution. On the one hand, Methodism does have a sense of rootage in the church of the ages with its traditions, forms, organizational patterns. On the other hand, early Methodism had its societies and fellowships for mutual witness and ministry; in later years Methodists have again recognized the place of smaller groups for study and worship and witness in depth. We have tried to adapt means to ends in the interest of meeting spiritual need. Thus, the church as fellowship and institution, as large congregation and smaller society, has been expressed. We are called to a continuing self-examination in our church life that we shall help maintain the vitality of the church both as fellowship and institution.

Who Is the Church? One of the missionary bishops, upon receiving new converts into the Christian faith and fellowship, makes this statement: "*You* are now the mission. *You* are now the church." This statement is in keeping with the approach of Acts, wherein the personal dimension of the church is stressed. To the question, "*Who* is the church?" we might reply that *the church is a fellowship of the seeking and the sharing.*

At the end of the second chapter of Acts we read, "And the Lord added to their number day by day those who were being saved." Is it not interesting that it does not say "the perfect" or "those who had arrived" or "those who were wise in all things"? No, it simply says, "those who were *being saved.*" The church is indeed a fellowship of those who are seeking and finding the new life of faith, hope, and love which God makes possible through Jesus Christ. Entrance into the church presupposes sincerity of purpose, a response in faith to the good news, a commitment of purpose and life. But it also implies a recognition of the need for "growth in grace."

John Wesley believed that the Christian life is a life of growth and "going on." [1] He was concerned that those who were newly born in the Christian faith should have "after-care." He thought of the societies and classes in relationship to Christian nurture. So, in our own time, we do well to recognize that persons within the fellowship of the church vary in the degree of their Christian maturity. But we are all seekers and we need each other in our spiritual growth and service.

Within the church seekers are also sharers. We are called to minister to each other. The church in

---

[1] See Olive Wyon, *Teachings Toward Christian Perfection* (Cincinnati: Service Center, 1963), p. 104; John Wesley, *Christian Perfection* (Cleveland: World Pub. Co., 1954), pp. 68, 104-5.

Acts was a fellowship of the concerned. So it must be today.

It is told that a lady approached following a service in a very formal church was asked, "Are you a stranger here?" "Why, yes," she replied, "I've been a stranger here for forty years."

Perhaps that is a bit of an exaggeration, but it does remind us that the church as *koinonia* is not a collection of strangers, but a fellowship of the concerned. This concern has to do not only with physical needs but with the deeper needs of mind and heart and spirit. Whatever our function in the church as institution, we are called to minister one to another. We come to church not simply to receive, but to share and serve in spiritual companionship.

One of the fundamental principles of Protestantism is the priesthood of all believers. Leaders of the Reformation had much to say about this, and this teaching is important today. The priesthood of all believers means (a) that we all have direct access to God; (b) that each person confronts God in his own right and responsibility—no one can have our faith for us; (c) each Christian is called to be a priest, in the sense of mediating Christ to his fellowmen. No persons or groups are to be regarded as *special* channels of grace; rather, as Luther put it: in his calling "every man may be useful and beneficial to the rest." Luther went on to say in his treatise on *Christian Liberty* that, by virtue of our Christian priesthood, "we are able to appear before God, to pray for others, and to teach one another mutually the things that are of God."

Along with the doctrine of the priesthood of all believers, Protestantism holds its own interpretation of Christian "vocation." All Christians are "called" into the life of faith and witness. Among those living in Christian faith there is no difference in status before God. One can be equally Christian in any useful calling.

The difference between clergy and laity is one of function. Every Christian is called to mediate Christ to his neighbor; indeed, Luther taught that every Christian can be a Christ to his neighbor.

The idea of mutual ministry within the Christian fellowship came to expression in the Methodist societies. John Wesley described a "society" as no other than "a company of men having the form and seeking the power of godliness, united in order to pray together, to receive the word of exhortation, and to watch over one another in love, that they may help each other to work out their salvation." [1]

Thus, those in the Protestant and Methodist traditions see the church as a ministering or saving fellowship—in which all are called to uphold and strengthen others in the Christian life. The church today, as in the beginnings of the Christian movement, is a fellowship of the seeking and the sharing.

Where Is the Church? We are accustomed to thinking of our church as located at a specific *place*. To be sure, the church building or buildings may be there, but where is the church? And when are we in the church? What we have said thus far suggests that

---

[1] John Wesley, *Works*, Vol. VIII, p. 267.

the church is built, not so much of stones and bricks and timber, as of the living relationships of persons— manifesting the Spirit of Jesus Christ. In Acts we have seen that early Christians came together for prayer and study—but they also went forth to witness, carrying with them a deep sense of the fellowship of which they were a part. Thus, to the question, "Where is the church?" we may answer that *the church is both gathered and scattered.*

Christian people come together for worship, the hearing of the preached Word, participation in the rites of the church—including baptism and Holy Communion—for study, the sharing of experience, mutual help. John Wesley sometimes spoke of "Christian conference." Christians come together to confer about the deep things of the spiritual life. They come together to confer about ways of applying or implementing their faith in deeds of witness and service. The church is a gathered fellowship.

But the church is also scattered. The church goes forth into the world through its organized services— such as hospitals, homes, social agencies, schools, and mission projects of various kinds. But the church also goes forth in those individuals who give living witness to their faith in the varied relationships and responsibilities of life in the home, school, work, community. But individual Christians do not go forth alone. They are a part of the universal church which unites all faithful followers of Jesus Christ (Heb. 12:1). There is great strength and inspiration in knowing that, even though we may be geographically alone, we are not alone spiritually. There is a "communion of saints" which transcends the boundaries of place and time. The church is present wherever persons live and work for divine ends in expressing their Christian commitment.

Thus we see that the Book of Acts has much to suggest to us, both about what the early church was, and what the church today is called to be. The church is fellowship and institution; it is composed of seekers and sharers; it is gathered and scattered. In all of this, the church is the instrument of God's continuing work in the world—called to proclaim, exemplify, and communicate the new life which God makes available to his human creatures everywhere.

FOUR:
the human side
of the church

IT HAS BEEN SAID THAT THE BEST ARGUMENT FOR Christianity is a Christian. The Book of Acts is full of interesting persons, enthusiastic in their faith, effective in their witness, calling us to a more vital Christian life.

As we have seen, Acts was not intended to be a biography or a series of biographies. Its main purpose is to interpret the mission of the church under the guidance of the Holy Spirit. Thus, we do not have complete reports of the careers of even its central figures—Peter and Paul. Rather, the persons mentioned pass in and out of the story in rapidly moving accounts. They are people in action, taking part in the unfolding story of the Christian movement. Here we meet some of the highly significant figures of the early church and through them we better understand the human side of the church's story.

The central characters are pictured as persons who

have personally experienced new life in the Spirit. In a number of instances they are radically changed persons. They find joy in their faith. They show courage in witnessing, often in the presence of opposition. They are deeply committed to the mission of the church.

We wish we had more information concerning many of them, and in some instances it can be gleaned from other New Testament writings. In the following pages we shall call attention to some of the persons of particular importance and then go on to consider the human side of the church in our own time. Some readers may wish to make a more extensive study of those here mentioned. (See Books for Further Reading, pp. 113-19.)

SOME IMPORTANT PERSONALITIES IN ACTS

Peter—First Leader of the Jerusalem Church. Peter is undoubtedly one of the most significant persons in the early church. His story, insofar as we have it, is an exciting one; his personality is fascinating; his influence, far-reaching.

Peter lived at Capernaum and was a fisherman when he left his work to become a disciple of Jesus. He was close to Jesus throughout his ministry and entertained him on occasion in his home. Peter is mentioned more than one hundred times in the Gospels. However, he seems to have been an impetuous and sometimes vacillating person. We are told that he fell asleep while on watch in the Garden of Gethsemane on the night of Jesus' arrest. While other disciples fled in fear, Peter joined the crowd at the trial, but when confronted with the charge that he was associated with Jesus, he denied knowing him.

We are told that it was this same Peter (Cephas) who was among the first to experience a vision of Jesus risen from the dead (I Cor. 15:5). Once remorseful for having denied his master, he now became a courageous witness to his Resurrection and preached with boldness.

Peter appears in the first chapter of Acts, calling for a successor to Judas. In the second chapter he is portrayed preaching his famous sermon at Pentecost, setting forth the apostolic message that Jesus has been made both Lord and Christ. In following chapters we read of Peter's varied activities in and out of Jerusalem. He is clearly the leader of the Jerusalem church, setting himself to the task of converting the Jewish people in Jerusalem to the new faith. If he had once denied Jesus, he now atoned for it in his courageous devotion.

Soon the sphere of his activity expanded. He engaged in missionary work to Jews outside of Jerusalem. With the expansion of Peter's work, James, the brother of Jesus, increasingly came to a position of leadership in the Jerusalem church.

An important part of Peter's story as set forth in Acts has to do with the issue pertaining to the relations of Jewish and uncircumcised Gentile Christians. Peter, who at first had regarded the "new covenant" as directed to Jews only—as is evident in his address on the day of Pentecost, when he addressed his hearers as "Men of Israel" (2:22, 36)—eventually became convinced (by the vision he received at Joppa, by the immediately following visit of the men sent from Caesarea by Cornelius, and finally by the gift of the Holy Spirit to Cornelius and his kinsmen and friends) that the gospel should be preached to Gentiles as well as Jews. Indeed, according to Acts, he remained in the home of Cornelius for "some days" (10:18) and ate with these uncircumcised converts, thus breaking the Jewish law. Taken to task by the Jews in Jerusalem, he defended his action resolutely (chapter 11) both on grounds of his vision and because of the granting of the Holy Spirit to Cornelius and his household.

Again in Acts, chapter 15, we find him taking a prominent part in the debate concerning the question as to whether Gentile converts should be subject to the rite of circumcision, and definitely declaring that "faith" and the bestowal of the Holy Spirit, not the observance of the Jewish rite, were the signs of God's acceptance of Gentile believers (15:8-11). He therefore concurred in the decision arrived at in Jerusalem and formulated by James.

There is nothing said in Acts about the dissension which apparently arose later and which Paul recounts vehemently (Gal. 2) where he accuses Peter of having eaten with uncircumcized Gentiles in Antioch, and then, on being criticized by James of backing down and "separating himself" from the Gentiles and eating only with Jews. According to James' thinking, Gentiles might enter the Kingdom of God through faith in Christ, but a distinction was to be drawn between Jewish Christians (the true inheritors of God's promise and calling) and uncircumcized Gentile Christians. They must not eat together. So James sent messages to Antioch; and Peter, with others, was persuaded.

It must be admitted that Peter's defection is in character. He was an impulsive person. But he was not one to hold stubbornly to a position when further information and experience indicated that he was mistaken. He came to a growing recognition that the idea of two kinds of Christianity—Jewish and Gentile—was not tenable. And so again he demonstrated his capacity for change and came to advocate the position that all those who are in Christ—Jew or Gentile—belong in one fellowship.

We do not have any letters written by Peter. (The Petrine authorship of I and II Peter is questioned by New Testament scholars.[1]) How we would treasure such letters if we had them today! However, many scholars believe that Peter's memories of Jesus became the basis of the Gospel of Mark.[2]

He passes from the scene in Acts without explanation. According to tradition he was executed about the year 64 in Rome among the Christians who suffered under Nero. For this tradition there is not conclusive evidence although it is certainly a possibility. He was prepared to give the last full measure of devotion.

In Peter we have an outstanding example of how a warm-hearted, impulsive man, combining human strengths and weaknesses, can become a new person

---

[1] Albert E. Barnett, *The New Testament: Its Making and Meaning* (Nashville: Abingdon Press, 1946), p. 215.

[2] Albert E. Barnett, *The New Testament: Its Making and Meaning*, p. 138.

through the impact of Jesus Christ upon his life, learning through experience, and becoming a mighty instrument of God's work in the world.

James—The Brother of Jesus. Although not one of the original disciples, James (perhaps the oldest of Jesus' brothers, Mark 6:3) came to leadership in the Jerusalem church. Probably his relationship to Jesus had something to do with his achieving this status, but of special importance was the fact that he was among those who witnessed to the Resurrection.

James held the Jewish law in respect. However, he was prepared to modify tradition as far as Gentile converts were concerned (15:13) in the light of God's action in Jesus Christ. He assumed special responsibility for work among the Jews, recognizing that Paul and some of his co-workers would carry on the mission to the Gentiles.

While Acts does not give us an extensive treatment of James and his work, we are helped to see him as another of the leaders of the early church, devoted to the Christian mission, anxious to be used in carrying on this mission under varied and changing conditions. According to tradition he was put to death shortly before the destruction of Jerusalem in A.D. 70.

Stephen—The First Christian Martyr. Only in the Book of Acts do we hear of Stephen. His appearance may be understood in the light of the author's interest in emphasizing Jewish-Gentile Christian tensions, together with the movement of Christianity beyond its original Jewish setting. Stephen fits into this pattern of interest.

66

In the sixth chapter we are told of the selection of seven men "to serve tables." Greek Christians complained that widows among them were being neglected in the daily distribution of food. Stephen, Philip, and five others, were named to correct this situation, enabling the apostles to carry on the "ministry of the word." Stephen is referred to as "a man full of faith and of the Holy Spirit." Of him it was also said that he was "full of grace and power." Charged with anti-Jewish bias, Stephen is brought before the council where he delivers the longest speech in Acts (7:2-53). The speech does not answer the charges brought against Stephen, but does make the point that Israel has rejected God's call in rejecting Christ. Stephen is then stoned—affirming his faith to the last. At the beginning of the eighth chapter we are told, "And Saul was consenting to his death."

In the picture of Stephen we have the portrait of a man of deep devotion, committed to the view that the Christian message was for Gentiles as well as Jews, who was willing to die for his faith. Remembering him we are reminded of the words of Tertullian: "The blood of the martyrs is the seed of the church."

Paul—Great Christian Missionary. Paul is the major figure in the Book of Acts even as he is one of the major figures in all Christian history. A Jew of orthodox parentage, he followed the Pharisees in his interpretation of the law. According to Acts Paul was born in Tarsus, was a Roman citizen, studied under Gamaliel in Jerusalem, and was present at the stoning of Stephen. After a period of crusading persecution of the Christians, he himself became a convert to the new faith (9:1-31). Always a man of great intensity, Paul now gave himself to the cause of Christianity with the same zeal he once manifested as its persecutor.

Paul became the leader of the mission to the Gentiles, although there were others who shared in this mission. Paul's major travels are frequently discussed in terms of three journeys, the first being described in chapters 13 and 14 of Acts, the second in Acts 15:36 through 18:22, the third in Acts 18:23 through 21:3. Paul's final journey, taking him to Rome for trial before the emperor's court, is described in Acts 27:1 through 28:16. Acts does not speak of the trial of Paul in Rome or of his death. According to tradition he was executed, thus joining the company of Christian martyrs in whose debt we all stand.

The gospel Paul preached was one of new life in Christ. He proclaimed individual and cosmic redemption through Christ who has overcome sin, death, and the demonic forces. Faith and new life are virtually synonymous in the thinking of Paul. There is a strong ethical emphasis in his message as he exhorts Christian people to live a life of purity and love. However, the Book of Acts has relatively little to say about Paul's actual message; we must glean that from his letters. Acts is more concerned with the *acts* of Paul as he takes his important place in the Christian mission.

We are indebted to Paul for many things. His insistence that Christianity is a universal religion was a matter of the greatest importance for future history. His emphasis on the life of faith in Christ, manifesting hope and love, has influenced subsequent generations of Christians. His thought of the church as fellowship (*koinonia*) with Christ and fellow-believers has guided later Christians in their thinking about the nature of the church. Christians together, he said, comprise "one body of Christ" (Rom. 12:5). His letters provide an invaluable source of insight into the Pauline churches, Paul's own thought, and varied aspects of early Christianity.

Paul was obviously a many-sided and complex personality. Deeply religious, he gave himself to his cause with seemingly unabating fervor. He was intense. He was a man of conflict in a period of conflicting ideas and cultures. However, even as he gives evidence of inner turmoil, he also manifests the deep resources and joy of Christian faith. He endured amazing hardships, including persecution, in courage and hope. He could be sharply critical of his opponents and intolerant of those who disagreed with him; yet he had a deep capacity for friendship and exhibited tender concern for those in need. Paul, indeed, was one of the giants of Christian history, and in his greatness we discern a deeply human person.

Barnabas—Devoted Church Leader. A native of Cyprus and a Hellenist Jew, Barnabas first appears in Acts 4:36-37 where we are told he sold a field and gave the proceeds to the apostles. One of the earliest Christians in Jerusalem, he is accounted among the apostles, although he was not one of Jesus' disciples. He vouched for Paul when the apostles first looked suspiciously upon him and his reported conversion (9:27). Apparently the leader of the Antioch church for a time, Barnabas was held in high regard by the apostles and other early Christians. In a number of instances his name precedes that of Paul in the reporting of various shared events (11:30; 14:14; 15:12).

A companion of Paul on some of his travels, Barnabas finally went his own way after differing with Paul as to whether John Mark should accompany them (15:37-38).

In Barnabas we have the example of another devoted adherent of the Christian movement who did much to extend its outreach at a crucial time. Like Paul, he seems to have combined a vision of the mission in its larger aspects with a practical sense of what needed to be done in the situation at hand. Later centuries of Christians are indebted to Barnabas, and others like him, who gave themselves so unselfishly in response to the good news.

Women in the Book of Acts. A distinguishing feature of Luke-Acts is the interest which is displayed in the part played by women in the early church. To be sure, the patriarchal form of family life is presupposed in the biblical writings. At the time that Acts was written women had achieved nothing like the status they have in our modern culture. We recall that Paul, taking for granted woman's place as subordinate to man's, insisted that women were not to speak in church (I Cor. 14:34-36)! In the light of all this, it is interesting to notice the numerous references to women in both Luke and Acts.

Of major importance is the fact that from the beginning the gospel was understood to be for both women and men. And from the beginning women shared with the men both in witnessing to their faith and in suffering for it. We are told that in his days of persecuting Christians, Paul turned upon both women and men (8:3; 9:1-2).

Let us now note those women in the early church who are mentioned in Acts. In Acts 9:36 we learn of Tabitha (her name in Greek being Dorcas) who lived at Joppa. She is described as "full of good works and acts of charity."

Mary, the mother of John Mark, is mentioned in Acts 12:12. We are told that a large number of Christians were meeting in her house for prayers when Peter came to them following his deliverance from prison. Here too, we have a reference to Rhoda the maid, who was so "overjoyed" when she heard Peter's voice, that she failed to open the gate for him and ran to announce his presence (12:14).

In Acts 16:13-15 an account is given of Paul and his companion speaking to a group of women at the riverside outside Philippi. Lydia of Thyatira, a seller of purple goods, responded to Paul's message and was baptized together with other members of her household. She said, "If you have judged me to be faithful to the Lord, come to my house and stay." The account goes on, "And she prevailed upon us" (16:15). In Acts 17:4 we are told that not a few of the leading women in Thessalonica responded to Paul's

71

teaching, and that in Athens a woman named Damaris was among those who believed (17:34).

Of special interest is Priscilla, the wife of Aquila, a Jew. According to Acts she and her husband were forced to leave their home in Rome, when the Emperor Claudius (A.D. 41-54) decreed that all Jews must leave the city. They made their way to Corinth where Paul met them on his first visit to that city. He stayed at their home and joined with them in the work they all shared as tentmakers (18:1-4). Paul stayed with them for over a year and a half, both preaching and working at his trade as tentmaker. After a period of time Paul went to Ephesus, Aquila and Priscilla accompanying him (18:18). In 18:26 we are told that Priscilla and Aquila talked to Apollos who "knew only the baptism of John," expounding to him "the way of God more accurately." It is interesting that the name of Priscilla precedes that of her husband in these accounts. Further references to Priscilla and her husband are found in Romans 16: 3, 4; I Corinthians 16:19; and II Timothy 4:19. The reference in Romans is of special interest because it says of these friends of Paul that they "risked their necks for my life," and that all the Gentile churches are said to be thankful to them.

THE HUMAN SIDE OF THE CHURCH TODAY

Great religion is like great music—it does not need defense so much as it needs rendition. That was true when the Book of Acts was written; it is true today. There is a deeply personal dimension in the faith and life and mission of the church. Its message is directed *to persons* in their life-situations; the truth of its transforming power is manifest *in persons* whose lives are changed; its mission of witness and service is carried on *by persons* who have committed their lives gratefully and gladly in response to the good news. Thus, human beings—individually and collectively—are of central importance in the life of the church. What is happening *to*, *in*, and *through* persons is the test of the church's ministry.

Good News for Human Beings. In every generation human beings seek courage, meaning, and wholeness in their lives. To the early Christians the gospel came as a life-transforming message. Through it they found greater courage and meaning and wholeness. Back of all that we read in Acts are the stories of human beings whose lives were changed. So it was that the early church felt compelled to go out in glad proclamation. Having experienced the reality of God's transforming work in Jesus Christ, early Christians went forth addressing themselves *to persons*.

If our modern church is to learn from Acts, it must keep this person-centered focus. The church is called to minister to all sorts and conditions of men—to all persons in need. Wherever there are human beings —of whatever race or nation or economic or educational status—there the church is called to serve by bringing its good news of hope in the living God. The church is not a fellowship of the comfortable or complacent. It is called to be a *ministering fellowship*, extending a welcome to those who are sincerely searching, witnessing to the new life of faith, hope, and love which is intended for all men. Important as statistics are, persons are more important; the church is called to *see persons*. Every local church is called upon to keep re-examining its inner life and program in the light of this calling—to minister to persons in need of God's good news.

Good News in Human Beings. Someone once said, "If you want to send a great idea—wrap it up in a person." That, of course, is of fundamental importance in Christianity. We believe that God's greatest good news was wrapped up in a person. We also believe that the truth of Christianity is confirmed in the lives of Christians who show forth from day to day the validity of the great claims of our faith. Lives *are* changed. New beginnings *are* made. Courage and meaning and wholeness *do* issue in lives which have once known spiritual defeat. Persons *do* find new understanding and strength and direction in the fellowship of the church. Christians *do* go forth in lives of witness, sometimes against great obstacles and at great personal cost. Christianity is much more than a theory or a memory. It is a living fact; it is good news *in* persons.

Of a great Christian it was said, "He lighted my candle." Is it not amazing how one person can light the candle of our best self? Is it not amazing how one person—living the Christian life—can give us strength and inspiration by what he is and does? Is it not amazing how one person—standing for what is right—can give *us* courage to stand for what is right? What tremendous help the early Christians must have received from the examples of men like Stephen and Peter and Paul. And so it has been across the centuries of Christian history. The truth of what Christianity affirms in words has been confirmed in human lives. And through the example of such lives persons have taken heart and been drawn into the higher life of faith.

Good News Through Human Beings. Someone once asked Sir Edmund Hillary how he happened to take up mountain climbing. He reported how as a boy he saw two veteran climbers returning from a long and difficult climb to the peak of a high mountain. They were apparently near exhaustion, but, looking into their faces, he saw a light which belongs to those who have known high adventure. Inwardly he exclaimed, "What a life!" And that day he determined to become a mountain climber. So it is with the power of example.

The best argument for Christianity is indeed a Christian. If we are drawn to the Christian life through authentic Christians, we, in turn, may be used to show someone else what the good news really is. The Book of Acts deals for the most part with the leaders of the early church. But it also makes clear how important to the life of the church were those persons of whom we know nothing but a name, and even those whose names we do not have but who were very much a part of the fellowship. Meetings were held in the homes of persons whose names we do not know. Work was done, decisions were made, services rendered, Christian virtues exemplified, examples given by persons unnamed. Yet, who can begin to measure the importance of the contributions made by these unnamed persons? The work of the church is carried on, not simply by the more conspicuous leaders, but by all faithful members of the fellowship.

In reading Acts, as well as other New Testament writings, one is likely to be impressed with the human strengths and limitations of many of the central figures. Paul spoke of having the treasure of the gospel in "earthen vessels." Thus it has always been. God's work in the world is carried on by persons who have human limitations—but who are dedicated in mind and heart and purpose. It is encouraging to us to know that God accepts and uses our creatureliness in carrying forward his saving work in the world. We all, wherever we are, may be instruments of the creating, redeeming, life-giving ministry of God.

FIVE:

the church in tension with the world

WHAT IS THE RELATIONSHIP OF THE CHRISTIAN church to the world in which it is called to serve? If the conscience of the Christian conflicts with the demands of the state, what ought the Christian do? To what extent should the church be subject to the controls of the state? Should the church be given protection and even special privileges by the state? To what extent is the church called to be a critic of government and culture? These are some of the questions with which Christian people have wrestled from the time of the rise of Christianity.

Today when changing situations require deepened study of current issues of church and state, it is appropriate that we should examine how one aspect of the problem of the early church's relationship to the Roman government was approached in the Book of Acts, and then consider the relationship of the church to the state and the culture in our own time.

RELIGIOUS TOLERANCE AND PERSECUTION IN THE FIRST CENTURY

Many Faiths—Religious Tolerance. At the time of Christianity's rise many religious faiths, groups, and movements existed in the far-flung Roman Empire. For the most part the attitude of the Roman government toward these varied expressions of religion was one of tolerance. To be sure, there were instances where "foreign" religions were looked upon with suspicion; but, in the main, the policy of the Roman government at the time of Christianity's rise was one of permissiveness toward the prevailing religions.

The earliest Christians were Jews and the Christian movement was generally regarded as being a part of Judaism. Since Judaism was tolerated by the state, the Christian movement was not at first challenged on legal grounds. We recall that Stephen, the first Christian martyr, incited to anger some who differed with his religious teachings, but he was not put to death by government decree but by the Jews.

It was with the growing importance of the state cult, with the attendant demand for emperor worship, that tensions increased between the early church and the government.

Christianity Under Persecution. The earliest opposition to the Christian movement did not come from government sources, but rather, from individuals and groups unfriendly to "The Way." Within Judaism, for example, there were those who did not regard the new movement with favor, who refused to accept it as a valid part of Judaism—and said so.

However, within a relatively short time, tensions developed between the Christian movement and government officials. For example, during the reign of Nero (A.D. 54-68) fire destroyed a part of Rome. Suspected of having started the conflagration himself, Nero placed the blame on the Christians, a number of whom were put to death. It is evident that at this time anti-Christian sentiment was sufficiently strong to make Christians convenient scapegoats. It was in Nero's reign also, according to tradition, that Peter and Paul were put to death.[1]

Later, probably during the reign of the Emperor Domitian (A.D. 81-96), the Roman state and Christianity came into open conflict. Some scholars believe that it was during this reign that Acts was written. Later still, probably during the reign of the Emperor Trajan (A.D. 98-117), though the precise date is not known, Christianity came to be regarded as an illegal religion, and profession of Christian faith was held to be a political crime, punishable by imprisonment, or even death.

This conflict between Christianity and the government grew out of the development of the state cult and the insistence on emperor worship.

The Roman Empire included a great variety of peoples—of many nations, races, and religions. The need to unite these people in loyalty to the empire and its rulers posed a major political problem and was intensified by frequent revolts led by local leaders during these years. To help solve this problem the

---

[1] James Hastings, ed., *Dictionary of the Bible,* pp. 220-21, 697, 1012.

state cult was encouraged—calling for the worship of the reigning emperor as well as his predecessors. Roma, the goddess who personified the city of Rome as well as the empire, was also made an object of worship.

Throughout the empire, shrines and temples were established with an official priesthood charged with supervision of the state religion. Gaius Caligula even tried to put his statue in the temple at Jerusalem, but he died before he could accomplish his project. Worship of the imperial gods was enforced under penalty of death. Thus, political loyalty was reinforced by religious sanctions.

Obviously these developments posed major problems for the Christians. For example, could a Christian participate in the rites of the state cult? Was it possible for one to give his highest allegiance to Jesus Christ and also engage in emperor worship? There were those among the Christians who did not think so. Thus the question became a pressing one—how should the Christian conduct himself when under pressure from the government to do what in good conscience he could not do? Because some Christians did hold back from the emperor worship there were Roman officials who looked upon Christianity with suspicion. Furthermore, as time went on, the relationship of Christianity to Judaism became less clear.

The Status of Judaism Before the Law. We have already noted that in its beginnings Christianity was regarded by its adherents and by Roman officials as a movement within Judaism. So long as this continued to be the case there was no serious problem of persecution by civil authorities. Even after the state cult developed to the point where emperor worship was demanded throughout the empire, Judaism enjoyed a unique status before the law. The government recognized Judaism as an ethnic religion which permitted its followers to worship only their own god. Thus, Jews were excused from worshiping the emperors, although they were required to make sacrifices *for* the emperors as a mark of their loyalty to the government.

Had Christianity continued simply as a movement within Judaism, there might well have been no major problem in its relations with the state. However, as we have seen, Christianity quickly moved beyond its Jewish setting. There was an aggressive mission to the Gentiles. During the lifetime of Peter and Paul there were already many non-Jewish Christians; by the end of the first century non-Jewish Christians were in the majority. With the growing awareness that the Christians were a separate people, government officials insisted that they be required to participate in the rites of the state religion.

Emperors varied in their attitude toward Christianity. Persecutions were sometimes sporadic and local, but many loyal Christians suffered and died for their faith. It was not until 313 that Constantine issued the Edict of Milan, making Christianity a tolerated religion. In the meantime, Christians wrestled with the problem of being true to their convictions in the midst of a threatening world.

Acts—A Treatise for Its Time. A number of New

Testament writings reflect early Christianity's difficulties with civil authority—Acts, Hebrews, Revelation, First Peter. All reflect the spirit of courage and hope in the midst of trying circumstances. All sound a clarion call to faithfulness in Christian witness.

It is probable that a major purpose, if not *the* major purpose, for the writing of Acts was to interpret Christianity in a favorable light to Roman officials. Among New Testament scholars there is widespread belief that Acts was written, not simply to tell a story or to record history, but to *make a case* for Christianity in the presence of mounting threats and persecutions.

The author of Acts uses an indirect method to achieve this aim. Instead of coming out with a direct appeal, he interprets the Christian movement as being the fulfillment of Judaism and as being divinely inspired and guided. He suggests that those who attack Christianity are actually attacking God. His method is subtle—but he wrote with great skill and deep conviction. If we endeavor to put ourselves in the time and place in which Acts was written, we begin to sense something of the deep concern which underlay the writing. No reader who is sensitive to the issues involved can be unmoved.

If one reads Acts with care, he will note three key ideas either explicitly stated or strongly implied:

(1) *Christianity is the true Judaism—the fulfillment of Jewish history and expectation.* The clear implication is that Christianity ought to be accorded the legal recognition which is accorded Judaism, even though it has now reached into the Gentile world. Thus, Christian leaders are portrayed participating in

temple and synagogue services, turning to the Scriptures with superior insight and reverence, affirming that Jesus is indeed the Christ, the long-awaited Messiah. Jewish-Christian controversies are interpreted as being "family quarrels" (18:14-16; 25:18-19). Paul argues that in preaching the resurrection of Christ he is actually taking his place beside those of his people (Pharisees and apocalyptic writers) who have affirmed belief in resurrection (23:6-9; 24:15; 26:6-8).

(2) *Christianity is not a subversive foreign religion —its leaders have been faithful to the state.* Much is made of the point that Paul was a Roman citizen, receiving considerate treatment on the part of Roman officials. Procurators and proconsuls sought to hear his message and refused to listen to his accusers; others kept him in custody for his own protection (13:12; 18:14-15; 24:22, 26; 25:25). The implication is, presumably, that all Christians should receive similarly considerate treatment.

In Acts 12:1-23 we find an account of persecutions which occurred under King Herod Agrippa I, a Jew, grandson of Herod the Great, who, according to the Gospel of Matthew, had ordered the massacre of the Innocents at the time of the birth of Christ. Herod Agrippa I "laid violent hands upon some who belonged to the church" and cast Peter into prison. Though he had received his governorship from the Roman emperor Caligula, he evidently persecuted Christians, not to curry favor with the Romans, but to "please the Jews." The story of Peter's marvelous deliverance (12:6-17) told with the brevity, excitement, and humor so characteristic of the narrative style of Acts, and the subsequent dramatic details of the death of Herod, are evidently intended by the author to demonstrate God's special protection of his Christian followers, and the fate of those who usurp the honor due only to God whom the Christians worship. In other parts of the book some Roman officials are depicted as having a deep interest in learning more of "The Way" (13:12). In other words, Christians are depicted as being worthy of respect and toleration within the empire.

(3) *Christianity is divinely inspired and directed.* Throughout Acts we find the emphasis upon the work of the Holy Spirit empowering and directing the early Christians. The Christian mission is God's mission. The Christians are God's agents. Under these circumstances it is most inappropriate for anyone to oppose the Christian movement; he might be opposing God himself (5:38-39). Again and again, as he delivers Peter, God intervenes to protect followers of "The Way."

In view of the emphasis placed in Acts on these basic contentions it seems highly plausible that the book was written against the background of increasing tensions between Christianity and the state, with growing threats of persecution. We ought to be grateful that early Christians faced up to this and other issues with courage and vision. We are called to face the important issues of our own time in a similar spirit.

CHURCH-STATE RELATIONS IN OUR TIME

To many of us living under democratic forms of government the problems encountered by first-century Christians may seem remote and of little concern. In the United States, for example, we take freedom of worship for granted. Unlike those living at the time Acts was written, we do not need to interpret our faith to government officials to avoid persecution. Nevertheless, issues which concern the relationships of church and state are very much with us. There are parts of the world in which freedom of worship is not a fact, and, even within democracies, there are vital issues of church-state relations with which we must come to grips. It may well be that the Book of Acts has more relevance for us in this area than we might at first assume.

Enduring Hardship for One's Faith. It is well for those in lands enjoying freedom of worship to recall that there are Christians in other parts of the world who live under much more difficult conditions. With the rise and spread of modern totalitarian governments the suppression of religious freedom has increased. In some instances the privilege of public worship has been curtailed. Christians have been persecuted again. In some parts of the world doors are closing to our missionaries; indeed, missionaries have been charged with subversion and have been imprisoned.

If there are tensions between church and state, there are also tensions within the religious world itself. With the resurgence of non-Christian religions, some of them missionary in character (Islam, Buddhism), Christians in some parts of the world do not enjoy the freedom they once did. In lands where governments have come under the control of authoritarian religious leaders, rights of minority religious groups have not always been respected. Thus, it is well for us to recall that there are parts of the world in which Christians labor under the opposition of government and religious forces. The courageous spirit and living faith reflected in the Book of Acts is needed today.

Separation of Church and State. The First Amendment to the Constitution of the United States, adopted in 1791, says in part: "Congress shall make no law respecting an establishment of religion, or prohibiting the free exercise thereof. . . ." According to Jefferson the intent of the clause against the establishment of religion by law was to erect a "wall of separation between Church and State." In the United States we have come to take the principle of separation of church and state more or less for granted, although in recent years this concept has been challenged in some circles.

The purpose of the founding fathers is clear. In the principle set forth is a recognition of the legitimate functions of both church and state. Man may have a dual citizenship, in church and state, with responsibilities to both. The state has the responsibility for keeping order and maintaining justice between man and man; the church is charged with specific religious responsibilities bearing on man's relations to God.

The principle of separation of church and state is designed to protect the integrity of both church and state. The state is not to encroach on the prerogatives of the church and the church is not to encroach on the prerogatives of the state. In theory, this seems desirable; in practice numerous problems rise. There are points of overlapping interest; it is at these points that tensions sometimes become evident. Those of us, who believe that the principle of separation of church and state is exceedingly important, must accept responsibility as both churchmen and citizens for learning more about the issues at hand. Our problems may not be precisely those of the first-century Christians, but issues of church-state relations are very much with us.

Present Problems of Church-State Relations. According to the principle of separation of church and state, freedom of worship and conscience is guaranteed. Religion is voluntary. One can belong to a church or not, as he chooses. This seems clear enough. However, in practice questions do arise. What shall be done if the teachings or requirements of a given religious group conflict with the regulations of the state? Shall the religious pacifist be exempt from military service? And who is to decide what is and is not a *religious* group? If the state makes this decision in reference to groups claiming tax exemptions or other considerations, is it usurping an authority it does not rightly have? Again, religious organizations in time take on institutionalized forms and sometimes seek legislation and special considerations in their own interests. To what extent is such action consistent with the principle of separation of church and state?

Many problems arise concerning the relation of

church and state in reference to *education*. Should federal aid be given to parochial schools? Should prayers and (or) Bible reading be permitted in tax-supported schools? Should religious festivals or holidays be recognized in public schools? Should courses in religion be offered in state universities, and if so, what kind? What of the principle of released time for religious education? Should certain teachings not accepted by some religious groups, such as the germ theory of disease and the evolutionary hypothesis, be permitted in public schools?

The issue of church and state also involves numerous questions which have financial implications. Should religious organizations be given special tax considerations? Should the government pay the salaries of chaplains in the armed forces or in governmental institutions? Should the state give financial aid to church-supported social agencies, hospitals, etc.?

If there are those who fear that the state may become too much involved in matters which are the church's concern, the question may also be asked how far the church is justified in moving into the affairs of the state. Is the church actually the "conscience of the community"? If so, is it called upon to criticize the policies of government on a moral basis? Is it justified in bringing pressure to bear for the enactment of legislation pertaining to gambling, temperance, housing, civil rights, censorship? What are the respective rights and responsibilities of church and state in the moral area?

Questions such as these make it clear that the issues of church-state relations are complex, even in a democracy. The concept of the separation of church and state is of great importance. The churches in America have thrived in many ways under this principle. However, we need to recognize that we must all assume the responsibilities of both faithful churchmanship and responsible citizenship in the state if this principle is to keep alive and vital. There are many continuing problems to be faced. The church cannot exist as "an island entire of itself." It must carry on its ministry in a complex world of many relationships. It is called to maintain its Christian integrity in a world in which there are many claims to our loyalty.

The Church in Tension With Culture. So long as the church is in the world it must deal not only with problems of relationship to the state, but also with the more inclusive problems of tension between the church and the prevailing culture. The church exists in a society often reflecting value systems and life-ways which differ from those for which it stands. Thus, problems are created for both the individual Christian as he faces choices involving belief and action, and for the church as an institution as it seeks to make policy-decisions in reference to its life in the world.

Many small religious groups have taken pride in being "different" from the world. They have held to beliefs and moral precepts which have sharply distinguished them from the rank and file of people. Some such groups have gone to the extreme of condemning the world as being utterly evil; they have refused to work seriously for human betterment; the emphasis of such groups has usually been other-worldly. The question emerges: How can the church "be different" and at the same time assume responsibility for constructive work in the world?

With the growth of the churches in the United States we have another situation emerging. Over 60 per cent of the American people now are associated with church or synagogue. Church membership has become the accepted thing. Many persons are admitted to church membership with little or no training for membership. The result is they have little understanding of what the church stands for. The thought that the church's teachings might be in tension with popularly held views and practices has not seriously occurred to them. The result sometimes is that church members do not seem different from anyone else. In some instances they are surprised and even critical when their church leadership takes a stand on religious and (or) social issues with which they are not in agreement. The fact that the church has a distinctive stance—grounded in the Christian understanding of God and man and life—has not been made clear to them.

A perceptive writer once observed that when 51 per cent of the people join the church, the church may be in trouble. He was pointing out that when the majority of the people become members of the church, the church may become simply a *reflection of culture* rather than a *leaven* within it. In a similar vein Dean Inge, twentieth-century Anglican prelate and scholar, once observed that in religion nothing fails like success. Thus, the church of today—particularly in a land where more and more people are church members—must face the problem of maintaining a creative tension with the world. Nothing is gained by pretending to be too good for the world, and little is gained by standing apart from the real issues of life while condemning the world. A church which stands for nothing in particular except "togetherness" is nothing more than one more social organization in the world. The church is called to be a leaven within culture, not just a reflection of it. It is called to be an instrument of the creating and redeeming work of God in the world. It is called to live in constructive tension with the world—giving living witness to reverence for life and devotion to the God of life. How to implement this theory in practice is one of the most crucial issues facing the church today. It leads us to a consideration of the mission of the church in our time.

SIX:

the mission of the church

WHAT DOES THE BOOK OF ACTS HAVE TO SAY ABOUT the mission of the church? It is inevitable that we should come at last to this important question. The early church, as portrayed in Acts, was a missionary-minded church. Indeed, the book is primarily an interpretation of the missionary expansion of Christianity. What relevance does this have for the church in our own time?

In every age there arises a temptation for the church to retreat from the world, to turn its attention exclusively upon itself, and ignore all outside it. There is, however, the opposite danger, namely, that the church become simply another organization within the world, reflecting the cultural matrix in which it exists. Does the Book of Acts offer any guidance in these matters? Does it suggest what the church is called to be and do in relation to the world? Does it help us better to understand the mission of the church in our own time? To such questions we now turn.

A Witnessing Church. In the eighth verse of the first chapter of Acts Jesus is quoted as saying to the apostles, ". . . you shall be my witnesses in Jerusalem and in all Judea and Samaria and to the end of the earth." This statement provides a clue to the spirit and purpose of the entire Book of Acts. From beginning to end it presupposes the witnessing, missionary character of the church.

In Acts the missionary outreach is not just an added interest or activity of the church; it is essential to the basic character and purpose of the church. To be a disciple is to be a witness, and to be a witness is to go forth with the good news of what God has done in Jesus Christ. Thus, Acts throbs with excitement and a sense of urgency about the church's calling. The church of Acts is no listless, self-contained, easy-going organization. It is a spirit-filled fellowship, empowered and directed to make a vital witness to the world.

Missionary Motivation. The Book of Acts makes it clear that motivation for the missionary effort of the early church is to be found in what God has done in Jesus Christ and in the continuing presence and power of the Holy Spirit. The God in whom "we live and move and have our being" now offers forgiveness, faith, and new life through Jesus Christ. The Christian is called to be a witness to the *living* Christ and an instrument of his abiding Spirit. Thus, the church's mission is God's mission. God is a missionary God.

We have already noted the important place which

94

the Holy Spirit plays in Acts. Pentecost not only marks the gift of the Holy Spirit; it also marks the beginning of the active missionary work of the church. The Spirit is indeed the inspiration and dynamic of the missionary movement. The Spirit instructs, guides, and inspires individuals engaged in missionary work.

In our own time we frequently hear discussions on whether the church should or should not carry on a program of missions. For the church portrayed in Acts this was not even a debatable question: discipleship implied witnessing and witnessing implied mission.

The Form of the Mission. The Book of Acts makes it clear that the missionary witness of the church takes various forms. First of all *the preaching of the word* should be mentioned. We are told that on the day of Pentecost Peter preached a memorable sermon, setting forth the claims of the Christian message and calling men to repentance and baptism. In his explanation of the Christian message and mission to Cornelius and his household, Peter refers to Jesus' commandment to disciples, "to preach to the people, and to testify that he is the one ordained by God to be judge of the living and the dead" (10:42).

As we have seen, there are numerous speeches and sermons in Acts. Indeed, they make up between one-fourth and one-third of the book. Much of this material is homiletical in character—proclaiming or heralding God's saving work through Jesus Christ. The longest recorded speech, as we have already seen, is that by Stephen (7:2-53). In Paul's missionary work preaching, of course, played a major part.

Along with preaching was *instruction*, designed to make clear the meaning of "The Way." It is evident, from several passages in Acts, that many who were impressed by the sermons of the apostles, were only convinced of the truth of the Christian message after they had discussed the evidence contained in the Scriptures. Teaching, therefore, was a significant part of the Christian mission. Paul and Barnabas spent a whole year teaching Christian converts in Antioch (11:26). Paul argued for three weeks with Jews at Thessalonica "explaining and proving" that Jesus was the Christ (17:3). Priscilla and Aquila undertook to expound to Apollos, "the way of God more accurately" (18:26-27).

The missionary program of the early church also included *deeds of service* to those in need. Numerous references are made to acts of kindness and mercy to persons in need of food and healing. It is significant that at the time Acts was written it was taken for granted that discipleship included an outreaching concern to be implemented in good deeds (2:45; 3:1-8; 4:34-35; 6:1-4; 8:7; 9:34, 36; 14:8-10).

We also learn that missionary outreach involved the *establishment of new churches* of those committed to "The Way." While we gain more insight into this aspect of the church's missionary program through the letters of Paul, Acts makes it clear that the organizational aspect of the early church's life had its important place and that there was a recognized need for extending the Christian movement through the establishment of new fellowship groups.

The deeply *personal aspect* of the missionary program is suggested in such a statement as that found in Acts 4:13. We are told that, having observed the boldness of Peter and John, their hearers "recognized that they had been with Jesus." Paul reports that, as a persecutor of Christians, he was present at the stoning of Stephen (22:20). Who can know what influence the courage and faith of Stephen may have had upon Saul? And surely the tireless dedication of Paul himself in later times must have been a major influence in the lives of many, turning them toward the One whose gospel he proclaimed in word and deed. Thus, it has always been. The Christian gospel is best commended and communicated by those whose very lives give witness to "The Way."

The Outreach of the Mission. In Chapter Three we noted the *inclusive* character of the church in Acts. This same characteristic of inclusiveness was found in the developing Christian mission. Such phrases as "to the end of the earth" (1:8) and "every nation under heaven" (2:5) suggest the range of interest and concern of Acts. The Christian mission was for all men, everywhere, regardless of distance.

We have also seen how the early church broke through the restriction of racial barriers, recognizing that the good news was for all persons. John Wesley's famous statement "The world is my parish" reflects the spirit of Acts where race, nation, economic status, and sex proved no insuperable barriers to the receiving of the good news.

The missionary emphasis of the early church is remarkable in the light of the fact that Christianity was a relatively small movement at the time, not infrequently experiencing opposition. How easy it would have been for those early disciples and followers of "The Way" to choose the path of retreat! But inspired as they were, they went forth in the face of difficulties and obstacles of many kinds to make a glad and vital witness.

We are told that on one occasion Paul was stoned and left for dead. But sustained and encouraged by disciples, he rose up and went on to Derbe with Barnabas. Then follow these words: "When they had preached the gospel to that city and had made many disciples, they returned to Lystra and to Iconium and to Antioch, strengthening the souls of the disciples, exhorting them to continue in the faith, and saying that through many tribulations we must enter the kingdom of God" (14:21-23). Such were the courage, devotion, and faith which made the spread and growth of the early church possible. We are the inheritors of the results of this devotion. How can we read such moving passages in Acts without asking deep and searching questions about the mission of the church in our own time? We who have received so much are now called to take our place in the company of those called to make a living witness "to the end of the earth."

THE MISSION OF THE CHURCH TODAY

The modern church has much to learn concerning its mission from the Book of Acts.

Vital mission inheres in a vital church and a vital

church is continually being renewed in its inner life. The church as portrayed in Acts was a fellowship in depth—manifesting the moving Spirit of God in the hearts and minds and relationships of its participants. The church was a people of God directing its attention to matters of ultimate importance. It had its human frailties in many ways, but it was concerned with divine matters and was disciplined and directed by the abiding Spirit of God. The modern church must know that its witness to the world—if it is to be effective—must spring from vitality of life within its own fellowship.

The Book of Acts also reminds us that the early church was alert to the events going on in the world about it. Indeed, the book itself, as we have seen, was intended for the eyes of Roman officials. It is sensitive to matters of government as they bear on the concerns of the church. Even though it was a "waiting community," living in expectation of the imminent return of Christ in judgment, it was aware of and concerned with the world at hand. While conditions have greatly changed in the intervening years, the need for the church to be alert to the nature of the world in which it functions has not changed. Today's church must learn all that it can about the factors that mold the lives of men today, seeking to speak relevantly about those things which are of ultimate concern. Christianity today cannot witness in the abstract but only in concrete life situations.

Again, Acts reminds us that there are no geographical limits to the church's concern and responsibility. The Christian mission is a world mission. This is just as true today as it was in the first century. However, the world is much more complex than it was in the first century. The modern church must wrestle with the profound questions of how to be relevant and effectively engaged in the world of the twentieth century.

Let us seek now to probe deeper into various aspects of the mission for which we are responsible if we are to accept the trust bequeathed to us by the early church.

Called To Be the Church. Strange as it may sound, the church's first mission is to itself. The church continually stands under the judgment of the living God. Our creedal formulations, our liturgies, our forms of administration, our ways of doing things, even our traditional views of what is right in a given situation must be continually re-examined in the light of the sovereignty of God and the mind of Christ.

The church is called to be the church of Jesus Christ. As such, it is an organization, but it is a very special organization. It is a fellowship, but instead of being just another group enjoying "togetherness," it is the fellowship of those who are seeking, finding, sharing, and *growing* in the new life God makes available through Jesus Christ (TEXT, pp. 51-54, 56). It is a fellowship of those who have found and are finding true freedom, but it is the freedom which springs from commitment to Him who is the Giver of Life. It is disciplined by the inner law of obedience to the Lord of Life rather than by the prevailing fashions of custom. It is a fellowship manifesting in its inner life the creating power and the redeeming love of God whereby men find a new life of faith, hope, and love. It is true to its calling only when it is the instrument of God's continuing redemptive work in the world.

However, the organized church is continually tempted to be *something other* than what it is called to be. Thus, there must be a continuing reformation, a continuing renewal going on in the inner life of the church. This involves worship, study, mutual ministry, service to the needy, and the continuing recognition, celebration, and dedication of life's basic experiences in the context of faith. It involves a continuing discussion within the church as to what the church is called to be and do. The church is a fellowship in which all participants recognize their responsibility in the total ministry of the church. There is a ministry of the clergy and a ministry of the laity—the differences are differences of function, but everyone who is truly in the Body of Christ has a ministry. Thus, there is a continuing examination of the total stewardship of ministry in the living church. The church now, as in the first century, is called to be open to the promptings and leadings of the Spirit of God ever with us to lead us into new truth and new areas of service.

A major function of the mission of the church today is the re-examination of itself to see whether it is indeed worthy to be called the Body of Christ. The church, like any individual, may sometimes fall into self-satisfaction and self-justification. Self-interest carried too far distorts the perspective of both individuals and organizations. The organized church forever stands under the judgment of the living God.

Not only must the church engage in self-examination in the light of its high calling in Jesus Christ; it must also listen to the criticisms which sometimes come from outside. To be sure, unjust and irrelevant criticisms have been leveled at the church in every generation, but sometimes perceptive observers outside the church see shortcomings in our witness which we ourselves do not always see, or which we are reluctant to acknowledge. In Protestantism we believe that the institutional church is a means to an end and not the final end itself. Therefore, we welcome just criticism from whatever source it comes.

The church is called to be authentic in its life and mission. It lives to make God real to men. It exists in the community to incarnate the life of faith. It is called to proclaim, exemplify, and communicate the hope and love which bring healing and new life. The will to witness and serve in the name of Jesus Christ is present wherever there is reality and depth of Christian experience. Lacking that experience there is no real sense of mission——at best, there may be attempts to send others to do what we ourselves do not care to do. We cannot have the fruits of mission without the roots. Thus, the mission of the church today begins with self-examination and inner renewal in depth.

If the life of mission is to be real, the church must exhibit in its own life the transforming power of God in the lives and relationships of its members, leading them to changed attitudes and genuine concern for social justice. Unless the church gives living testimony to the truth it proclaims in word—providing a spiritual and moral dynamic in our time—others will write off the Christian message as just pious talk.

A Mission Near and Far. One of the great needs of the church is to come to a more realistic image of mission itself. How many church members there still are who associate the word "mission" with the sending of "foreign missionaries" to distant lands to talk to inferior people in an inferior culture about an otherworldly salvation! We need to bring up-to-date our concept of mission in the light of actual world conditions, the struggle for independence and self-determination in emerging nations and civilizations. Somehow we must learn that mission means more than the financial support of specific projects or activities. *Mission is the total outreaching witness of the church and churchmen, near and far.*

Strangely enough, there are some church members who are quite willing to contribute to missionary work in Africa, India, or South America, yet are quite indifferent to the human need or injustice which exists in the next block. On the other hand, there are those who see no reason for extending the Christian mission beyond the local scene "when there is so much work to be done right here at home." Such attitudes reveal lack of insight into the concept of mission itself. The Christian mission is the life of glad and grateful witnessing—near and far—in the name of One whose Spirit transcends all barriers of distance, race, and nation (1:8; 11:18; 13:46).

A Mission for All Life. Paul Tillich, one of our contemporary theologians, has reminded us of the importance of correlating the Christian message with our actual situation. In a similar vein we might say that the Christian witness is irrelevant if it does not throw light on the meaning of life in its concreteness. What shall be the gain if we proclaim the sovereignty of God and the lordship of Christ but fail to communicate their relevance for the daily life of man?

Dr. Harry Overstreet once told the story of seeing some seemingly ordinary rocks for sale in a shop. Detecting Dr. Overstreet's bewilderment that such rocks should be on sale, the proprietor invited him into a back room which was in total darkness. There he threw an ultra-violet light upon the rocks, and immediately colors of indescribable beauty came forth. So, the living gospel, incarnate in persons, reveals new meaning and depth in work, play, human relations, and all experience. When the light of God's presence, purpose, and power is thrown upon life, all things are different. A depth and significance we had missed before becomes apparent.

The church in witnessing to its allegiance to Christ is called upon to deal with the major experiences of life, including crisis situations. It must relate its witness to crucial problems which arise in family life, business, life on the campus, work in all its forms, citizenship, and issues in our society involving justice. Too often the church fails to be as effective as it ought to be, simply because it deals overly much with generalities. The mission of the church involves coming to grips with questions as to how the gospel is to be implemented in specific situations, often ambiguous in nature. The church must show the relevance of its message at those crucial points where life sometimes breaks down and at those points where the possibility of new meaning exists.

A Mission in Changing Times. In the 1870's a bishop was talking one day with the president of a small college. The bishop expressed the view that everything of importance had now been invented or discovered. The educator disagreed, saying, "I predict that within fifty years men will fly like the birds." The bishop was shocked. "Flight is reserved for angels," he said, "and you are guilty of blasphemy!" It is interesting to learn that the name of the bishop was Milton Wright. Back home he had two young sons, named Wilbur and Orville!

The world is indeed in rapid change. This age of space necessitates more adequate interpretations of man, the human situation, the universe. An important part of the mission of the church is to help men find a faith for living in the space age. Dr. Harlow Shapley, the astronomer, has reminded us that a one-planet deity no longer will do. The church must give leadership in men's search for more adaquate concepts of God. It must help men in their search for understandings to undergird a faith capable of disciplining and directing men in an age of power. The church must be prepared to enter into conversation with scholars in all fields and to receive new information. It must encourage research and scholarship. It must undergird the educational dimensions of the church's life, recognizing that Christian education goes on as long as life goes on. The mission of the church involves consideration of men's doubts and questions, serious consideration of men's ultimate concerns. The vital church must encourage inquiry and discussion as men seek the truth of God in a new day.

As he returned from outer space Major Gagarin exclaimed, "How beautiful is our earth!" Looking at the same view, Colonel Glenn shouted, "Man, that view is tremendous!" It may well be that the realization that we share "one world," and that creation is indeed a thing of surpassing wonder, will contribute to a new sense of human solidarity. There is a spiritual dimension to our explorations of outer space.

At the same time, we must recognize that a closer look reveals much that is not beautiful on our earth. Man's inhumanity to man is a fact. Injustice is a fact. Inexpertness in the art of human relations is a fact. The increasing depersonalization attendant upon growing mechanization and organization of life is a fact. It is in a world where such facts are present that the church must make its witness.

The church is called to give religious, intellectual, moral leadership in a time when there are major conflicts of ideas and values and when the way ahead is not always clear.

If the church cannot always give a simple blueprint to be followed, it *can* speak to the great issues; it *can* keep alive awareness of the moral factors involved; it *can* speak for the dignity of all men; it *can* keep proclaiming that all life must be lived under the sovereignty and claim of God; it *can* undergird persons and institutions as they seek the way which expresses true reverence for life.

Thus, it is the responsibility of the church to be authentically involved. And it is the responsibility of the local church to permit its leadership to speak, in the name of Jesus Christ, to the deep issues of life, including controversial issues. The vital church is marked not so much by agreement on all issues as by the conviction that it must be relevant to changing times—to all of life where fundamental values are involved. Together we must seek the Christian way. Sometimes the working of the Holy Spirit is manifest in the midst of those who seek light on difficult problems. Sometimes the Holy Spirit is present in the honest sharing of differing points of view. Sometimes God works through creative interchange. Thus, the church should make provision for study, discussion, and creative interchange on the part of its members.

A Mission of Leaven. We are told that Jesus said, "To what shall I compare the kingdom of God? It is like leaven which a woman took and hid in three measures of meal, till it was all leavened" (Luke 13: 20, 21). The church serves no constructive purpose by pretending to be too good for the world and by withdrawing from it or hurling denunciations at it, nor by becoming so completely identified with the culture in which it exists that it has no word of judgment to bring. The church is called to be in the world, but more than a reflection of the world. It is called to love the world, but always to live in creative tension with the world. It is the mission of the church to be a leaven in the larger loaf of society. Thus it bears witness to the living God and to his kingdom.

It is the mission of the church to provide a "frame of orientation and devotion" within which an individual's personal duties become important. It is the mission of the church to witness to God's active presence in history, to call forth the moral strengths of men, to serve as conscience in the community, and to communicate a transforming vision which lifts human beings above the trival and mean.

It is the mission of the church to reveal the superficiality of much of today's "togetherness" by demonstrating true depth of heart, mind, and spirit in its own fellowship. Only a fellowship of depth and integrity can be true spiritual leaven.

A Mission of Varied Forms. A relevant witness to and in the world must take a variety of forms. If the good news is to come to persons as being good news *for them* the church must learn and practice the arts of identification and communication. It must enter into the lives of persons in such ways that life's highest possibilities are revealed in the light of the gospel.

Let us note four forms or expressions of mission through which the Christian witness becomes relevantly engaged in the world. First, there is the mission of *Christian example.* If there is indeed a "new being" or "a more excellent way," it must be demonstrated in human lives. The best argument for Christianity is a Christian. Emerson observed that "what you are speaks so loudly I cannot hear what you say." Life speaks to life. For professing Christians *to be*

Christian in their varied relationships is the first expression of mission.

The second form of mission follows directly from the first. It is that of *rendering service to those in need*. The church of Acts was a fellowship of the concerned. It must ever be so. Love of God and love of neighbor go hand in hand. A pastor friend once told me that he once made a hospital call on a young man from a distant community whom he had never met. The young man could not comprehend that a total stranger would come to see him to extend a hand of friendship and concern. "But why did you come to see *me*?" he kept asking. A world all too familiar with ways of human exploitation for personal gain sorely needs the witness of a concern that reaches out. It is through such practical concern, expressed on the human level by man to his neighbor, that many persons have come to understand and trust the larger concern of God.

The third form of mission involves *verbal communication*. Preaching which sets forth the claims of Christian faith calling men to make response; instruction which seeks to clarify the meaning of Christian faith and to nurture the life of faith; conversation with interested persons to the end that there may be a continuing dialogue with the world—all these are forms of verbal communication. As travel increases and there is ever greater intermingling of the peoples of the earth, it is imperative that the church recognize the need for entering into conversation with persons of varied faiths and value systems. The policy of aloofness will not do. The church is called to make explicit just what it is and just what it stands for.

The fourth form of mission is that of *Christian social action*. As the world becomes more highly organized and our lives are increasingly influenced by various power structures, it is essential that the church make its witness in the area of social action. At the same time that it seeks to bind up the wounds of those who have been hurtfully exploited on the highway and left beside the road, it must exert influence that the conditions on the highway shall be improved and that justice shall be undergirded.

A church that has no social witness to make is not an authentic Christian church. The church must bear corporate witness to the world; it must speak out on issues of religious and moral significance, enter into discussions of policies and their implementation, encourage such social action as is indicated by Christian ethics, send forth its members to take their place in the community as responsible Christian citizens. It has been said that the church has two functions: one is to comfort the afflicted and the other is to afflict the comfortable. Where there is authentic Christian witness there is the mission of Christian social action.

These various forms of mission can and should be expressed in and through the local congregation. They should be implemented by those agencies of the church which are responsible for administering mission work around the world. Obviously situations vary in the opportunities which are afforded for making Christian witness. But wherever Christians are present, there is opportunity for some one or more of the forms of mission we have considered: Christian example, service to those in need, verbal communication, Christian social action.

A Mission Involving the Whole Church. As we come to the close of our study of Acts we confront one of the central lessons of this great biblical book—to be a Christian is to be involved in Christian mission. Christian mission is not to be carried on only by a few persons who are assigned to this task. Although there are varieties of responsibilities, *all* Christians are called to give their living witness. Mission involves the whole church.

Thus, remembering the heritage which is ours, each one of us might well ask, "What is the nature of *my* participation in the continuing mission of Jesus Christ?" We are all called, not only to receive, but to witness to the spiritual blessings of Christian faith and life.

If we are inclined to think that our lives are unimportant and our influence insignificant, we do well to recall that God has a way of using rather ordinary people for divine ends. The Book of Acts gives evidence of that. Along with the more conspicuous leaders like Paul and Peter were the unnamed Christians who were so essential to the life of the early church. Paul himself spoke of having the treasure of the gospel "in earthen vessels." We cannot do everything but everyone of us can do and be something. How faithful we are in that calling may be far more important to other human beings than we can possibly know. "So we are ambassadors for Christ, God making his appeal through us" (II Cor. 5:20).

BOOKS FOR FURTHER READING

for *Acts: Then and Now*

Helpful information on the Book of Acts and the church today will be found in the following works, which may be ordered from the Cokesbury Book Store serving your territory if in print (prices are subject to change). Your local church, public, or college libraries may be able to lend "out-of-print" books to you. *Editor.*

COMMENTARIES ON ACTS AND HISTORICAL BACKGROUND

BARCLAY, WILLIAM. *The Acts of the Apostles.* Rev. ed.; Philadelphia: Westminster Press, 1957. $2.50.

BARNETT, ALBERT E. *The Modern Reader's Guide to Acts.* New York: Association Press, 1962. Paper, 50 cents.

BARNETT, ALBERT E. *The New Testament: Its Making and Meaning.* Rev. ed.; Nashville: Abingdon Press, 1946. $3.50.

BLAIKLOCK, E. M. *Commentary on The Acts of the Apostles.* Grand Rapids, Mich.: Wm. B. Eerdmans Pub. Co., 1959. $3.00.

BROWN, STANLEY C. *Evangelism in the Early Church.* Grand Rapids, Mich.: Wm. B. Eerdmans Pub. Co., 1963. $2.00.

BRUCE, F. F. *The Book of Acts.* Grand Rapids, Mich.: Wm. B. Eerdmans Pub. Co., 1954. $6.00.

BULTMANN, RUDOLF. *Primitive Christianity in Its Contemporary Setting.* Cleveland: World Pub. Co., Meridian, n.d. Paper, $1.55.

CADBURY, HENRY J. "Acts of the Apostles," *The Interpreter's Dictionary of the Bible.* Nashville: Abingdon Press, 1962. (See Vol. 1, pp. 28-42.) 4 vol. set, $45.00.

CADBURY, HENRY J. *The Book of Acts in History.* Naperville: Alec R. Allenson, 1955. $3.50.

CADBURY, HENRY J. *The Making of Luke-Acts.* 2nd ed.; Naperville: Alec R. Allenson, 1958. $5.00.

DIBELIUS, MARTIN. *Studies in the Acts of the Apostles.* New York: Chas. Scribner's Sons, 1951. Out-of-print.

EASTON, B. S. *Early Christianity: The Purpose of Acts and Other Papers.* Frederick C. Grant, ed. Greenwich, Conn.: Seabury Press, 1955. Out-of-print.

FILSON, FLOYD V. *The Three Crucial Decades.* Richmond, Va.: John Knox Press, 1963. $3.00.

GOODSPEED, EDGAR J. *An Introduction to the New Testament.* Chicago: Univ. of Chicago Press, 1937. $5.00.

GRANT, ROBERT M. *Historical Introduction to the New Testament.* New York: Harper & Row, 1963. $5.00.

KEE, H. C. & YOUNG, F. W. *Understanding the New Testament*. New York: Prentice-Hall, 1957. Text edition, $8.50.

LADD, GEORGE E. *The Young Church* (Bible Guide, No. 15). Nashville: Abingdon Press, 1964. $1.00.

MACGREGOR, G. H. C. & FERRIS, THEODORE P. "Acts; Romans," *The Interpreter's Bible*, Vol 9. Nashville: Abingdon Press, 1954. $8.75.

MOULD, ELMER W. K. *Essentials of Bible History*. Rev. ed.; New York: Ronald Press Co., 1951. $6.00.

O'NEILL, J. C. *Theology of Acts in Its Historical Setting*. Greenwich, Conn.: Seabury Press (S.P.C.K.), 1961. Out-of-print.

WILLIAMS, C. S. C. *The Acts of the Apostles*. New York: Harper & Row, 1958. $4.00.

HOLY SPIRIT AND THEOLOGY

BARRETT, C. K. *The Holy Spirit and the Gospel Tradition*. New York: The Macmillan Co., 1947. Out-of-print.

BULTMANN, RUDOLF. *Theology of the New Testament*, Vol 1. New York: Chas. Scribner's Sons, n.d. $4.00.

GRANT, F. C. *Basic Christian Beliefs*. Cincinnati: Service Center, 1960. 75 cents. New York: The Macmillan Co., 1961. Cloth, $2.95.

HENDRY, GEORGE S. *The Holy Spirit in Christian Theology*. Rev. ed.; Philadelphia: Westminster Press, 1965. $3.50.

HODGSON, LEONARD. *Doctrine of the Trinity*. London: James Nisbet & Co., Ltd., 1943. Out-of-print.

ROBINSON, H. WHEELER. *The Christian Experience of the Holy Spirit*. New York: Harper & Bros., 1928. Out-of-print.

SCOTT, ERNEST F. *The Spirit in the New Testament*. Garden City, N.J.: Doubleday & Co., n.d. Out-of-print.

VAN DUSEN, HENRY P. *Spirit, Son and Father*. New York: Chas. Scribner's Sons, 1958. $3.50.

THE CHURCH AS FELLOWSHIP AND INSTITUTION

BARCLAY, WILLIAM. *New Testament Wordbook* [meaning of 15 Greek words]. New York: Harper & Row, 1957. $2.50.

BROWN, ROBERT MCAFEE. *The Significance of the Church*. Philadelphia: Westminster Press, 1956. $1.00.

DE DIETRICH, SUZANNE. *The Witnessing Community: The Biblical Record of God's Purpose*. Philadelphia: Westminster Press, 1958. $3.75.

DEWOLF, L. HAROLD. *Theology of the Living Church*. Rev. ed.; New York: Harper & Row, 1960. $6.00.

GUSTAFSON, JAMES M. *Treasure in Earthen Vessels*. New York: Harper & Row, 1961. $3.50.

HARKNESS, GEORGIA E. *The Church and Its Laity*. Nashville: Abingdon Press, 1962. $3.50.

MINEAR, PAUL S. *Images of the Church in the New*

Testament. Philadelphia: Westminster Press, 1960.
$6.00.

NIEBUHR, H. RICHARD. *The Purpose of the Church
and Its Ministry.* New York: Harper & Row, 1956.
$2.50.

WELCH, CLAUDE. *The Reality of the Church.* New
York: Chas. Scribner's Sons, 1958. $3.95.

THE HUMAN SIDE OF THE CHURCH

BONHOEFFER, DIETRICH. *The Cost of Discipleship.*
2nd ed.; New York: The Macmillan Co., 1963.
Paper, $1.45.

ENSLEY, FRANCIS G. *Paul's Letters to Local Churches.*
Nashville: Abindgon Press, 1957. $1.00.

HUNT, CLARK W. *Living in the Light of the Cross.*
Nashville: Abingdon Press, 1964. $2.75.

JAMISON, ALBERT LELAND. *Light for the Gentiles:
Paul and the Growing Church.* Philadelphia: Westminster Press, 1962. $1.50.

KEPLER, THOMAS. *The Fellowship of the Saints*
[Anthology]. Nashville: Abingdon Press, 1948.
$7.50.

THE CHURCH IN TENSION
WITH THE WORLD

[1] AULT, JAMES M. *Responsible Adults for Tomorrow's
World.* $1.00.

BARNES, ROSWELL. *Under Orders: The Church and
Public Affairs.* Garden City: Doubleday and Co.,
1961. $2.95.

BENNETT, JOHN C. *Christians and the State*. New York: Chas. Scribner's Sons, 1958. $4.50.

BERGER, PETER L. *The Noise of Solemn Assemblies*. Garden City: Doubleday and Co., n.d. Paper, $1.95.

HERBERG, WILL. *Protestant—Catholic—Jew*. Garden City: Doubleday and Co., 1955. Paper, $1.45.

LENSKI, GERHARD. *The Religious Factor*. Garden City: Doubleday and Co., 1961. Paper, $1.45.

[1] MUELDER, WALTER G. *Power Structures, Ethical Concerns, and the Church in the World*. 15 cents; 10 for $1.25.

[1] *Pray for World Leaders* (UN Prayer Card). Free.

SANDERS, THOMAS G. *Protestant Concepts of Church and State*. New York: Holt, Rinehart, and Winston, 1964. $7.50.

SOLBERG, RICHARD W. *God and Caesar in East Germany*. New York: The Macmillan Co., 1961. $4.95.

THE MISSION OF THE CHURCH

ANDERSON, GERALD. *The Theology of the Christian Mission*. New York: McGraw-Hill, 1961. $6.50.

The Christian Mission Today. Edited by Board of Missions of The Methodist Church. Nashville: Abingdon Press, 1960. $2.25.

[1] JONES, TRACEY K., JR. *Our Mission Today*. Cincinnati: Service Center, The Methodist Church, 1963. $1.00.

KRAMER, HENDRIK. *World Cultures and World Religions*, The Coming Dialogue. Philadelphia: Westminster Press, 1961. $6.50.

PARKER, ROY P. *The Church on the Move*. Nashville: Tidings, 1964. 60 cents.

WARREN, MAX. *The Christian Mission*. New York: Friendship Press, 1951. $1.50.

WEBBER, GEORGE W. *The Congregation in Mission:* Emerging Structures for the Church in an Urban World. Nashville: Abingdon Press, 1964. $3.50.

WILLIAMS, COLIN W. *Where in the World?* Changing Forms of The Church's Witness. New York: National Council of Churches, USA, 1963. Paper, 75 cents.

[1] Order from SERVICE CENTER, 7820 Reading Road, Cincinnati, Ohio 45237.

ANALYTICAL—Concerned with the examination of the parts or elements which compose a substance, or a writing, or text.

APOCALYPSE—A revelation, a prophetic disclosure or announcement of the ultimate reign of God; literature written in the belief that the Second Coming of Christ was imminent, such as The Revelation to St. John.

APOCRYPHA—Writings of doubtful authenticity or authorship; the fourteen books of the Septuagint which are not found in the Hebrew Bible, and are regarded by most Protestants as not canonical.

Apocryphal Works—Non-canonical writings; religious writings of uncertain origin, not included in the Old or New Testament.

APOLOGY—A written or spoken argument or defense of an action or doctrine.

Apologetic—Explanatory, or defensive speech or writing.

CANON—The books of the Bible; the collection or list of books accepted by the Christian church as genuine and inspired by the Holy Spirit.

Canonical Gospels — The four Gospels, Matthew, Mark, Luke, and John, which were included in the New Testament Canon, having been accepted by the Christian church as authoritative as early as the second century.

COSMOS—The world or universe, an orderly and harmonious system, the opposite of chaos.

Cosmic—Characteristic of the cosmos, hence vast, immeasurably extended in time and space.

DIACONATE—Deacons or deaconesses; or the office or body of deacons.

"EARTHEN VESSELS"—Ordinary people, liable to imperfections, flaws, and weaknesses. (Vessels made of clay were used for cooking or serving ordinary daily meals, whereas temple vessels were brass or precious metals.)

ECCLESIA—Translated, church; Greek word meaning a meeting or gathering; the term acquires religious associations in the New Testament and is used to signify a gathering for a particular religious purpose; a company called into being by God through Christ; a chosen people—the renewed Israel; the body of Christ or the people of God; a Christian congregation; the company of those who have received the gift of the Holy Spirit.

ECUMENICAL—Universal, united; pertaining to the whole Christian church as in the World Council of Churches.

ETHNIC—Native; pertaining to a race or group having a common and distinctive culture.

GLOSSOLALIA—"Speaking in tongues," the utterance of ecstatic words or sounds, frequently inarticulate, under the influence of religious excitement or fervor.

HELLENIST—A Greek-speaking Jew. In the early church the Hellenists bridged the gulf between Jew and Gentile.

Hellenistic—Relating to the Greek character, spirit, or civilization.

HERESY—Religious opinion differing from the authorized beliefs or standards of a particular church.

HOMILETICAL—Pertaining to preaching; having the characteristics of a sermon or homily.
Homily—A religious discourse or sermon; a moralizing discourse.

INDIGENOUS—Native, natural to a particular place or thing.

KOINONIA—Fellowship, such as a Christian fellowship or body of believers; suggests having something in common, an association, communion, close relationship. Brotherly unity; conveys idea of fellowship with the Holy Spirit; a close relationship with the gospel; unity and inner harmony of Christian groups.

The PETRINE Authorship—Authorship attributed to the Apostle Peter.

PROCONSUL—Governor or commander over a Roman province having powers like those of a consul who was one of the two chief magistrates having power over the ancient Roman republic and empire.

PROCURATOR—A Roman officer appointed directly by the emperor to collect taxes in a conquered territory and to curb sedition.

RITUALISTIC JUDAISM—Legalistic Judaism; the strict observances of all the ceremonies and laws initiated by Moses and by the priests who followed him.

SANHEDRIN—The supreme Jewish council of 71 members in Jerusalem during post-exilic times. It originated as 70 elders appointed to assist Moses in government. It was reorganized by Ezra after the Exile for a largely judicial function. By Roman times it was a legislative council largely responsible for the government of the country, but it could not pronounce the death sentence without the sanction of a Roman procurator. Called a "court of justice," "senate," "council of elders," it was an aristocratic institution presided over by a hereditary high priest.

THEOLOGY—The study of God and God's relation to the world and man.
Systematic Theology—The attempt to set forth the major doctrines and teachings of the Christian church in a systematic way, to show the grounds on which they rest, and to make clear their relevance for the human situation.

TORAH—The five books of Moses; the pentateuch; divine instruction, law.

"WE-PASSAGES"—Passages in which an author uses the first person plural as if he, himself, were present at the events he records.

PRONUNCIATIONS

Ananias ......AN-ah NY-as
Antioch ......AN tee ock
Apollos ......ah POLL os
Aquila ....ah quil ah
Areopagus ...ahr ih OP ah guss
Artemis ......ARE teh miss
Barnabas .....BAR nah bahs
Bithynia .....bih THIN eh ah
Caesarea ....SEZ ah REE-ah
Capernaum ...kah PURR nay-um
Constantine ..KON stun tine
Corinth ......KOR inth
Damaris .....dah MAR riss
Damascus ....de MAS kus
Derbe ....DUR bee
Diaconate ....dye ACK kon-it
Domitian .....doe MISH ann
Ecclesia ......ih KLAY-zih-ah
Elijah ....ee LIE jah
Elisha ....ee LIE shah
Elymas ......ell ih mahs
Ephesus ......EFF ih sus

Galatia ......gah LAY shah
Gamaliel .....gah MAE lih ell
glossolalia ...gloss so LAY lee-ah
hellenist .....HELL en ist
Iconium ......eye KOE neh um
Dean Inge ....ing
Joppa ....JOPP ah
koinonia .....coin-ah NEE-ah
Lystra ....LISS trah
Matthias .....mah THY us
Petrine ......PEA TRINE
Pisidia ....peh SIDD eeh ah
presbyters ....PRES bi terz
Procurators ...PRO cue ray-tors
Proconsuls ....pro CON suls
rabbinic ......ra BINN ick
Sanhedrin ....san HEE drin
Tertullian ....turr TULL ih ahn
Theophilus ...thee OFF-eh-luss
Thyatira .....thigh at TIE-rah
Paul Tillich ..TILL-ick
Trajan ......TRAY jahn

Pronunciation of a few of the words in the text is provided here for the convenience of the reader. If there is any need for further information, dictionaries may be consulted.—*Editor.*

NOTES ON THE COVER

The "Church at Gelmeroda" by Lyonel Feininger. Asked
what the painting on the cover of this book means to you,
you might answer with a single word: "Aspiration." And
you would undoubtedly be near the truth, close to the intention
of the New York artist, Lyonel Feininger (1871-1956),
whose preoccupation with soaring diagonals and rays of light
and their symbolic meaning is evident in many of his works,
particularly in his "tall canvasses" of churches and houses.

Lyonel Feininger studied violin with his father, a noted
violinist and composer, and began participating in concerts
at 12. At 17 he went to Europe to study art. He began to
support himself as a newspaper cartoonist working in Berlin
and Paris and later for the *Chicago Sunday Tribune* where he
drew "Wee Willie Winkie's World." Feininger's political
cartoons gained some notice, but his concern with over-all
forces rather than with detailed particulars led him to re-
nounce the cartoons.

The photograph on the cover is a reproduction of Feininger's
painting, the "Church at Gelmeroda." Gelmeroda is a small
Thuringian village, near Weimar, Germany (the town made
famous as the home of the poet Goethe). This church, with
its amazing tower which—according to tradition—has never
been struck by lightning, is said to have been in existence since
the fifteenth century. It made an immediate and deep impres-
sion on the young artist when, shortly after World War I,
along with Paul Klee and Kandinski and other now famous

artists, he became an instructor at The Bauhaus, a newly founded school of arts and crafts in Weimar. Many of Feininger's compositions and drawings of the church are in existence; of 13 for oil paintings, 10 have been painted. Some of the blues and greens of the "Church at Gelmeroda" are reproduced on the cover. To these colors the artist added burnt siennas, yellow-greens, and other muted jewel-tones. The Metropolitan Museum of Art in New York City, to which we are indebted for permission to reproduce the painting, acquired the "Church at Gelmeroda" in 1942, after the artist had returned to settle permanently in New York.

Lyonel Feininger was fascinated by churches, standing alone or surrounded by houses. He used their "aspiring verticals" and their "gravitating horizontals" as a "means to demonstrate the theme of rising and falling, or ascending and descending. The dramatic tensions increase in rich modulation to the point where the diagonal forms, becoming steeper, lead up to the vertical of the tower which disentangles itself from the confusion of houses and rises into freedom. The forces of the airy heights gather around the tower and like a sheltering roof embrace church and houses." [1]

A fellow-artist once said, "Feininger begins from nature, out of which he extracts a spiritual essence in the fullness of time." [2] He concentrated on the individual's response to forces beyond himself showing how man seeks freedom from the isolation of his own overstressed individuality.

"He made the space-creating forces beyond the individual form the basis of his composition. . . . The difference between material and immaterial is no longer of significance. Light and shadow, for instance, become as important as solid bodies. . . . The different planes of actuality combine and merge in one single plane. . . .

"The constellation of these forces have infinite possibilities. Their rays merge and create hills and mountains. . . . Embracing again, they produce houses and skyscrapers . . . [in] utmost simplicity. His energies are devoted to the creation of a space in which the universal forces, absolute and free, manifest the reality of their ordered being. . . . He had discovered a higher truth in nature, he had discerned in it the symbol of man's being and striving." [1]

"There is a new understanding of relationships. Blank spaces are part of a composition, like rests in music." [2] Commenting on Feininger's painting of the "Church at Gelmeroda" and his other paintings of churches, a critic has observed: ". . . We can imagine organ tones, the polyphony of a fugue by Bach, the ringing sound of church bells. The tower stands guard; and at the same time it reaches upward. It is a symbol of man's striving toward security and freedom." [1]

"Feininger's art is compact of opposites: on the one side reticence, withdrawal and discipline; on the other, sensibility and human warmth." Contemporaries noted his preoccupation with the phenomenon of light. It is the play of light and shadow in this picture which lines out its planes and gives it its structure. "It is a light tended in a dark age; an act of will or devotion." [2]

After further reflection you may decide that the word "aspiration" alone is insufficient to capture the meaning of the "Church at Gelmeroda." Another word is needed to express motivation of man's loftier thoughts, prayers, and actions—both within and without the structured church. That word is "Inspiration."—*Editor.*

[1] Alois J. Schard, "Lyonel Feininger," *Lyonel Feininger* [and] *Marsden Hartley*, edited by Dorothy Miller (New York: The Museum of Modern Art, 1955), pp. 14-18. Used by permission.

[2] Frederick S. Wight, "Lyonel Feininger," *Jacques Villon, Lyonel Feininger, with Reflections on Painting* by Jacques Villon (New York: Chanticleer Press, published for Institute of Contemporary Arts, Boston, 1950), pp. 29-33. Used by permission.

THE RISE OF CHRISTIANITY

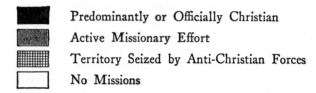

- ■ Predominantly or Officially Christian
- ▨ Active Missionary Effort
- ▦ Territory Seized by Anti-Christian Forces
- ☐ No Missions

Reprinted from the map, "The World Mission of The Methodist Church" (Service Center, 7820 Reading Road, Cincinnati, Ohio 45237), 72 x 42 inches. Folded, $1.00; in mailing tube, $2.00.

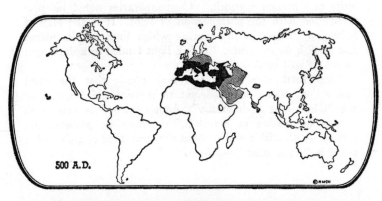

500 A.D.

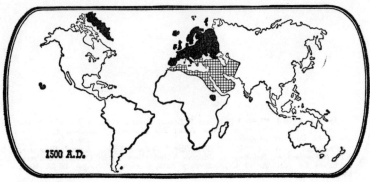

1500 A.D.

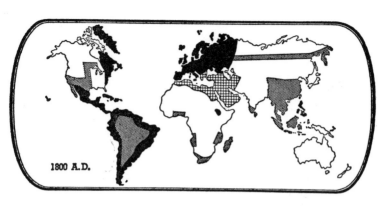

1800 A.D.

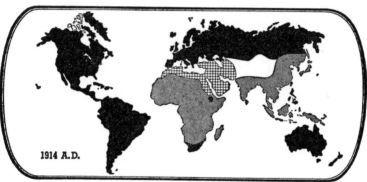

1914 A.D.

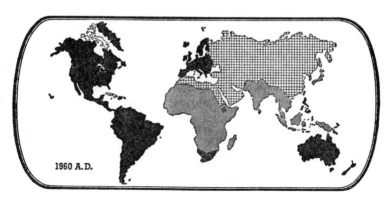

1960 A.D.

Prepared by:
Editorial and Literature Department
Joint Commission on Education and Cultivation

Order from

SERVICE CENTER
BOARD OF MISSIONS—THE METHODIST CHURCH
7820 READING ROAD
CINCINNATI, OHIO 45237
PRICE: $1.00

FE465